New York Times bestselling author

TERESA GIUDICE

With Heather Maclean
Photographs by Steve Legato

Fabulicious!

ON THE GRILL

New York Times bestselling author

TERESA GIUDICE

With Heather Maclean
Photographs by Steve Legato

Fabulicious!

ON THE GRILL

Teresa's **Smoking Hot**
Backyard Recipes

RUNNING PRESS
PHILADELPHIA · LONDON

© 2013 by Teresa Giudice
Photographs © 2013 by Steve Legato

Published by Running Press,
A Member of the Perseus Books Group

Books published by Running Press are available at special discounts for bulk
purchases in the United States by corporations, institutions, and other organizations.
For more information, please contact the Special Markets Department at
the Perseus Books Group, 2300 Chestnut Street, Suite 200, Philadelphia, PA 19103,
or call (800) 810-4145, ext. 5000, or e-mail special.markets@perseusbooks.com.

ISBN 978-0-7624-4977-4
Library of Congress Control Number: 2013935106

E-book ISBN 978-0-7624-4986-6

9 8 7 6 5 4 3 2 1
Digit on the right indicates the number of this printing

Cover and Interior design by Frances J. Soo Ping Chow
Edited by Jennifer Kasius
Food Styling by Debbie Wahl
Prop Styling by Marieellen Melker
Typography: Affair, Archer, Baskerville, Bodega Sans, La Portentia,
Neutra, Samantha, Sweet Rosie, and Swingdancer

Running Press Book Publishers
2300 Chestnut Street
Philadelphia, PA 19103-4371

Visit us on the web!
www.runningpresscooks.com

Fabellini is a registered trademark of Fabellini Brands, LLC.
Nutella is a registered trademark of Ferrero SpA.
Baci is a registered trademark of Perugina.

Dedication

We're so lucky we get two kinds of family:
the one we're born with, and the one we make ourselves.

This book is dedicated to all of you, my friends and fans,
my second family. Your constant support means the world to me.

Grazie di tutto! Ti amo, ti amo, ti amo!

ACKNOWLEDGMENTS

I want to acknowledge the amazing people
who help make everything possible:

My juicy husband Joe, my beautiful daughters Gia, Gabriella, Milania, and Audriana, my wonderful parents Antonia and Giacinto Gorga, my fantastic co-writer and friend Heather Maclean, the world's best agent Susan Ginsburg, culinary master Rick Rodgers, the entire team at Writer's House and Running Press, especially Jennifer Kasius, Chris Navratil, Allison Devlin, Craig Herman, and Frances Soo Ping Chow, photographer Steve Legato, Debbie Wahl, Marieellen Melker, my photo co-stars Priscilla DiStasio and Edyta Keska, and all my other family, friends, and fans.

Thank you for filling my life with love.
I adore you all more than you'll ever know.

Contents

Chapter 4

Insalate e Minestre
(Salads and Soups)

Chapter 5

Carne (Meat)

Chapter 6

Pollo (Chicken)

Chapter 7

Pesce (Seafood)

Chapter 8

Pasta

Chapter 9

Contorni (Side Dishes)

Chapter 10
Dolci (Desserts)

Hot-Hot-Hot!

Chi mangia bene, vive bene.

"Who eats well, lives well."

Everything about Italy is hot: the climate, the people, the fashion, even the shape of the country—how much hotter can you get than a tall boot with a high heel?

Everything about Italians is hot, too—and not just on the outside. We're hot blooded. We are famous for our passion and our tempers, for our love and our loyalty. And when it comes down to it, we just like things hot. We like our partners hot; we like our weather hot; and we *love* our food hot.

If you've read any of my previous cookbooks, you know red pepper flakes are one of my favorite ingredients because I love to eat hot. If you've seen me on *The Celebrity Apprentice* or *The Real Housewives of New Jersey*, you know that I find myself in hot situations far more often than I'd like. (Every time I try to get out, they keep pulling me back in!) But both of my parents are from Italy, and I was conceived in the "old country," so at least I come by my heat honestly.

I absolutely love-love-love the summer. I love when it's hot outside. Maybe it's because I love to be outside. The winters—especially the ones we've been having lately on the East Coast—are not my friend. When it's cold, everyone seems to hibernate. We hide in our houses. We hide our bodies under layers of clothes.

When it's hot, there's no hiding. You have to face yourself and your neighbors and your body . . . and that's an amazing, happy thing! To me, there's nothing

English is my second language. I grew up speaking Italian first. It was all that was ever spoken in our house. I still speak Italian exclusively with my parents, and sometimes with my husband, brother, and kids.

Not being a native English speaker, I do make mistakes sometimes when I'm talking—usually when I'm thinking in Italian and trying to translate to English. The biggest problem I have is with English sayings, idioms, and proverbs that I didn't grow up with because I have never heard them and don't have a lifetime of references for them. So "Jekyll and Hyde" comes out as "Heckyll and Jive" because I didn't grow up hearing about these two British guys (or one guy?) . . . like most Americans don't know who *Il commissario Montalbano* is. (Inspector Salvo Montalbano is a famous detective from Italian books and TV shows, kind of like the Italian Sherlock Holmes.)

Since our sayings are totally different in Italian—and just as fun!—and almost all have to do with food or cooking, I thought that in this book I'd teach you some of them. We'll start with this one: *U defiette da pignate u sa sul u cuocchiare.* It literally means "only the spoon knows the inside problems of the clay pot," and is the Italian way of saying "never judge a book by its cover." A great lesson for us all!

better than sitting in the warmth, surrounded by family and friends, with the delicious smell of food sizzling on the grill and a cold drink in your hand—just relaxing. The rest of the year, holidays and homework have us all running around like crazy. But in the summer, we can finally kick off our shoes and really enjoy our blessings.

One of my biggest blessings—besides my four beautiful daughters and my incredible family—is that I get the opportunity to share my family's authentic Italian recipes with you. I am so humbled and honored to be writing my fourth cookbook! That the first three have all been *New York Times* bestsellers blows my mind. But it really shouldn't because I know I have the best fans in the entire world.

You guys are sexy, smart, and you don't miss a thing. I wish I could have a big, fabulous summer party and invite all of you! I can give you the next best thing, though: a book full of my summer party favorites.

In just a few chapters, you'll become a grill god/goddess, learn ancient Italian secrets of cooking delicious and juicy food over an open flame, and unleash your own inner hot Italian. I've also adapted some of the most popular recipes from my previous cookbooks so that they can be cooked on the grill. Think you can't make lasagna or chicken Parmesan or pizza on the grill? Think again!

So fire up the grill, pop open a bottle of Fabellini, and let's get this party started!

CHAPTER 1

Get Out of the Kitchen: Grilling 101

Amicizie e maccheroni, sono meglio caldi.
"Friendships and pasta are best when they are warm."

I adore summer food. Unlike in the winter when even our food hides in cans and under thick creams, summer food comes out to play. Everything is fresh, crisp, colorful, and extra healthy. The farmers' markets are open; the produce section of the grocery store is overflowing; and we're spoiled for choice: avocados, berries, eggplant, figs, grapes, green beans, peas, peppers, peaches, plums, summer squash, tomatoes, watermelon, zucchini (my favorite), and tons more. They're all my favorites, actually, especially when they're in season, inexpensive, and outrageously delicious.

There's a saying in Italy: *Pesche, fichi, e meloni sono migliori quando sono in stagione.* It means "peaches, figs, and melons are best when they are in season." It's used as a proverb to explain that "everything has its time," but it works literally as well because it's true: things taste so much better when they're in season. Think about a tomato. Sun-ripened and picked fresh from a local vine, they are sweet, tangy, zesty, and meaty. Grown in a hothouse and shipped across the country during winter months, they are tasteless, slimy, and—*Madonna mia!*—mealy.

Out-of-season and out-of-state-grown food doesn't just taste worse, it also doesn't cook as well, and isn't as good for you. Hothouse or imported produce has to be harvested before it's ripe, after which it is chilled, transported, stored, transported again, handled by multiple people and machines, and sometimes even treated with chemicals and/or radiation to give it the correct color (and sometimes an artificial shine) and to protect it from a world of germs. The premature picking and long journey means that the food doesn't have as many nutrients as it could, and it also loses moisture. Dense produce like apples can handle the trip better, but something soft and vulnerable like a tomato has no chance. This is why, during the summer, I buy as many fresh tomatoes from farmers' markets as I can, why my family cans hundreds of jars of them every August, and why, if I'm out and in a pinch, I'll go for canned tomatoes over winter pickings in the produce department every time.

SEXY GRILLING

I also adore the way we cook summer food because grilling is healthier, sexier, and keeps the heat out of your house. For starters, you can't really grill super unhealthy foods. Anything fatty or extra processed, like a Twinkie, is not going to work. It will melt or dissolve back into the mess of chemicals it came from. To stand up to the high heat and wide spaces on a grill, food needs to be real, solid, and raw.

Grilling food is also healthier because you are essentially burning the fat off of it. When food is fried or even baked, it sits in its own oil and absorbs the oil that you added to the pan. The higher heat also means grilled foods generally have a shorter cooking time, which means that veggies lose less of their precious nutrients.

Finally, my favorite part of grilling is that you can do it in your bikini. It's not only sexy, but also great for weight maintenance and weight loss. Preparing and eating food in a bathing suit is a great way to keep you motivated to eat healthy and exercise, and naturally keeps you from wanting to eat too much. I heard once that if you really want to lose weight, you are supposed to eat in your underwear. Not very practical, but it keeps you accountable. There's no hiding your "yummie tummie" when you're staring at your belly button between bites. That might sound extreme, but swap it for your swimsuit and surround yourself with good, positive friends, and you may just find the kick start you've been looking for. In fact, if you start right now—eating healthy food and moving your bones—you can look even more amazing by the end of the summer.

GRILLING VS. BARBECUING

Believe it or not, I am positive this is not the best barbecue book that you'll ever buy. Why? Because it's not a barbecue (or barbeque or BBQ) book at all. It's a grilling book. Although some people use the words "grilling" and "barbecue" interchangeably, there is a difference.

They are both methods of cooking food over an open flame, but, technically, when you barbecue something, you cook it at a low temperature for long, long time; when you grill food, it's hot and fast. Barbecued food, like pulled pork or beef brisket, depends on smoke and rub flavors and lots of sauce to give it its signature tender taste. It's mostly done in the South and over charcoal or wood fires. Grilling, which we do in Italy, uses the heat from a grill to cook, but not really flavor the food, like chicken, seafood, steak, and vegetables. That's where we come in!

A SUPER SHORT HISTORY OF ITALIAN GRILLING

Until World War II, outdoor grilling in America was usually reserved for camping trips. We'd moved our cooking indoors years earlier, and pretty much kept it there, except for regional practices like barbecue in the South. After the war though, people moved from the cities to the suburbs and had space. Big backyards meant big parties, and cooking outside became cool again. Small, round charcoal grills called braziers, which didn't have vents or covers and blew ash into your face, were the only portable option until the first Weber kettle grill was introduced in 1952. Hamburgers, chicken, and steak rejoiced.

Cooking those foods inside generally involved frying in butter, but a pan full of butter didn't translate well to outdoor grills. All of that smoke sort of took the fun out of outdoor parties, so people looked around for new ways to season their otherwise plain meats. Most people turned to the South for grilling inspiration, using sticky, sweet barbecue sauces slathered over their food.

Italian-Americans, however, didn't need to find a new way since their food preparation could remain the same indoors or out. Italians—especially in rural areas like Sala Consilina in Salerno, where my family is from—have cooked on outdoor grates over open fire for thousands of years, and still continue to do so. The Mediterranean marinades, herbs, and flavors using a few simple ingredients like olive oil, garlic, rosemary, and basil, work just as well on the grill as in a pan. That light, delicious, healthy style is what I'm honored to be able to pass along from my family to yours.

CHARCOAL VS. GAS

While the first modern commercial grills were charcoal—and charcoal is still quite popular—I'm a gas grill girl. I love the convenience, the temperature control, and the cleanliness (or "cleansiness," as I famously said on *The Real Housewives*) of a gas grill. You heat it up and get cooking. That's it. With a charcoal grill, you have to deal with a heavy bag of briquettes, getting them lit and then waiting around, making sure you've used enough briquettes and in the right place, building the perfect fire, and more often than not, you and your food end up covered in black stuff. (I like to wear black as much as the next girl, but preferably with a hot necklace and some designer heels.) In short, charcoal grills are extra work, and I'd rather spend that time with my kids and my company. So in my family, we cook on a gas grill. I'm going to assume you are too.

If you're not, though, to cook over charcoal, just pay attention to your heat. If your charcoal grill has a thermometer built into the hood, you're good. If not, use the hand-over-the-fire trick: if you can hold your hand just above the grate for three seconds, you have medium heat. If you can only last one or two seconds, your grill is too hot. Let the coals settle down for fifteen minutes, and check again.

---

* * * Keep a Lid on It * * *

If you only remember one piece of grilling advice, let it be this: *Keep the lid closed!* Just like an oven, every time you open the lid, you're letting heat escape, throwing off the cooking temperature, prolonging your cooking time, and possibly ruining your food. I know it looks cool to stand over an open fire, but dry, overcooked food won't make you anyone's hero. Save the flame licking for s'mores.

TURN ME ON

If you are already the grill master of your domain, feel free to skip ahead to the next section, but for those of you who are grilling virgins—maybe you're in college, maybe you just got your own place, or maybe you've secretly been afraid that you'll blow up the whole block—I'm going to take it nice and slow. After reading this book, you'll know all the culinary secrets to delicious grilled food, but that won't matter if you don't even know how to work your appliance.

I don't care if you have someone in your life who "mans" the grill for you, no girlfriend of mine is going to just prep and then stand there and look pretty while someone else cooks the food. (Unless of course, that's your gig. And then I say, more power to you!) But seriously, that person might be out of town or stuck in traffic, and relying on someone else to even get the grill going could end up wrecking your entire meal, or worse, your party. So keep reading, baby doll!

The first step: turning the grill on. It might seem crazy to talk about something so basic, but this is a safe place: no judgment and no shame. Modern grills aren't as intuitive as stoves or ovens, and there is something just a little scary about a tank full of gas and a button marked "ignition." But in truth, there really isn't much difference. Stoves and ovens have their own source of heat, you just can't see them as well as on a grill. You'll hear me say this again and again, but a grill is really nothing more than an outside oven. And unless you're made of gingerbread, there's no reason to be afraid.

Of course, every grill is different, so please take a few minutes to read your owner's manual. But in general, here's all you need to do:

1. Make sure your grill is in a nice, open ventilated area. Not too close to the house (I have a friend who melted the vinyl siding off his house!), and not indoors or in a garage.

2. Open the lid before turning on the gas valve. Very, very important to make sure that the gas can't build up in there.

3. Turn the valve on the tank or natural gas line one full turn counterclockwise, to the left. (Remember for almost anything that screws, it's "lefty-loosey, righty-tighty." And keep your dirty jokes to yourself!) You don't have to unscrew it until it stops; just one full turn is enough and will make it easier to shut off quickly.

4. Turn just one burner control knob—whichever one is closest to the ignition switch—to high.

5. Press the ignition switch. If the burner does not light, turn it off, turn the gas off, wait for the gas to disperse, and then try again. If the burner lights, turn the other burners on to high. Close the lid and let it preheat for ten minutes.

Don't forget to turn the grill off after you're done cooking! But first, remove the food, turn the burners up to high, close the lid, and then set a timer for five minutes to let the stuck-on food burn off the grate and to clear the burners. Then turn the gas valve all the way clockwise ("righty-tighty") until it stops, and finally turn off the burners (this will ensure you don't have any gas trapped in the hoses). This is the perfect time to clean your grill with a grill brush since the food residue will be nice and soft. Then leave the lid open and let the grill cool down completely before you cover or move it.

✷ ✷ ✷ Safety Dance ✷ ✷ ✷

—Just like in your kitchen, you should have a fire extinguisher outside near your grill for any emergencies.

—Never store extra gas tanks near your grill.

—Keep your long hair and any flowing summer dress or long sleeves away from the grill, as they can easily catch fire.

SCRAPE & LUBE

There is nothing yuckier than seeing someone grill on a dirty grate. Why would you want old black bits of food from last week sticking to your new food? Keeping your grill grate clean is a must—a must for the health of your grill, the health of your guests, and the health of our friendship! And, besides, a clean grill will give your food those super sexy grill marks.

Cleaning your grate is super easy, and you only need one thing to do it: a long-handled, stiff wire brush made specifically for cleaning grills. That's it! You don't need special cleaning spray or anything else; in fact, adding chemicals to the place where you cook your food probably isn't a great idea. The brush alone will do the

> ### ✱✱✱ Hookup Checkup ✱✱✱
>
> Every time you hook up your grill to a gas tank, check the connections for leaks. Make sure all burners are turned off, then turn the gas line on, and brush all connections with soapy water. If any bubbles form, you have a leak. Turn off the gas, let it disperse, and then undo and reattach the connections.

trick. (And, as my mother would say, just a little *olio di gomito*—or elbow grease.)

Make sure you scrape the grill clean before and after each use. If you make it a habit to brush the grill after cooking while it's still hot, you shouldn't have to do much to clean it before the next time.

Also, don't use any kind of lubricant—even cooking oil—to grease the grate before putting the food down. I hear that recommendation a lot, and it's garbage. You're only wasting the oil and encouraging flare-ups. Instead, as you'll see in my recipes, we oil the food or let a wet marinade discourage any sticking to the grill.

TOOLS OF THE TRADE

You will need a few basic tools for grilling. You might already have some of them in your kitchen. But if you can, keep your grilling stuff together in a toolbox or something like that. And don't buy one of those grilling tool sets—the ones you might think about getting for Dad on Father's Day with handles that look like baseball bats or golf clubs—because they are more attractive than they are useful. (I know a few men like that. . . .)

Here's what you'll need:

Long tongs: This will be your main turning tool, so it should be easy to use. Get a good set of heavy-duty tongs with wide gripping ends. Look for ones that have locking mechanisms to keep the tongs closed during storage.

Wide, thin spatula: Kind of like what you would turn pancakes with, but be sure your metal grilling spatula has a long handle so you can reach to the back of the grill to flip your burgers.

Grilling brush: You want a sturdy, long-handled metal brush made specifically for scrubbing the gunk off of the grill before adding the food and after you're finished grilling.

Basting brush: A long-handled (do you see a trend here?) brush is the best kind so you can reach all over the grill. Silicone brushes are much easier to clean than the old kind with natural bristles.

Oven mitts or potholders: Keep a pair to use just while grilling because they tend to get dirtier from soot than the ones you keep in the kitchen.

Instant-read thermometer: This little guy has a thin metal probe to insert into the food, which works a lot better than the large stem of the old-fashioned thermometer. The instant-read part is important because you want a fast readout to keep the handle from melting. You don't keep this kind of thermometer in the meat while it's cooking, just insert, check, and pull out.

Perforated grilling pan: Some thin foods can fall through the grate, and delicate ones can stick to the grate. That's when to use this indispensable tool, which sits on the cooking grate to hold the food in a single layer. Looking like a cross between a small frying pan and a colander, grilling pans have replaced grilling baskets for their ease of use and cleaning.

Metal skewers: For *spiedini* (the Italian version of kebabs), the food is cooked on skewers. A lot of grilling experts recommend bamboo skewers, soaked in water before adding the food, but the wood still burns! You can find metal skewers at just about every supermarket, and they're reusable, so you'll save money over time. You don't need a fancy set because the food comes off the skewer for serving anyway, and no one will see it. That being said, the metal skewers with flat blades do the best job of holding the meat in place.

Chimney starter (for charcoal grills only): This metal canister helps ignite briquettes without the need of messy lighter fluid. You put the charcoal in the top part, a couple of sheets of newspaper in the bottom part, light the paper, and that's it. In about fifteen minutes, the coals will be tinged with white ashes, and you can dump them out of the canister (use a pot holder because the handle is hot!) into the bottom of the grill, and get started cooking.

THE INS AND OUTS OF GRILLING

Most of us learned how to grill like this: throw food on grill, and cook until done. You have more control than you think, though. You can actually grill food two ways: using direct heat and using indirect heat.

Direct heat used to be the only way people grilled. You turn the burners up, place the food directly over the fire, and cook the hell out of it. It's only really good for food that can be thoroughly cooked in less than fifteen minutes though— any longer and you've burnt the outside before the inside is done. You also have to really watch the fat dripping onto the flames, as that's what causes dangerous flare-ups.

Indirect heat is when you cook food not directly over the fire, but next to it, using the heat rather than the flames. To cook using indirect heat, you would turn on all your burners to preheat the grill, then turn one or two of them off, usually in the middle, and put your food over the unlit burners. The result is juicy perfection. Believe me, some grill masters use indirect heat more often than direct! Don't think you have to char something to make sure it's done on the inside. Here's the solution: think of your grill as an outdoor oven.

Ovens use indirect heat. The entire space is heated, and you trust that your food is going to cook in there just fine. And you don't bake everything at 500°F

✳ ✳ ✳ A Great Grill Buying Guide ✳ ✳ ✳

If you're really just starting out or need a new grill for any reason, here are a few tips to help you get a fabulous one. I called a friend who's worked with Weber Grills for years, and here's what he told me:

Price

How much you spend is up to you. You can get a great little grill at the basic level. It's the add-ons (side stove-style burners, work stations, illuminated lids so you can see in the dark, natural gas hookups, and so on) that make the price add up.

Extra Side Burners

The one extra I recommend, if you can afford it, is at least one extra stove-like burner on the side of the grill; the little kind for kitchen pots. I use mine all the time for prepping food, as you'll see in the recipes.

Type of Metal

Bigger gas grills can sometimes be found with tons of bells and whistles but low prices because they've skimped on one thing: the type of metal that makes up most of the unit. Cheaper metal might not matter to you if you live in a perfect climate, but we grill a lot at the Jersey Shore, where the salt air can eat up a cheap grill in no time. If you want long-lasting, look for a grill that is made of heavy gauge, high-quality stainless steel and ask a lot of questions of your neighborhood vendor. The salesperson will guide you towards a reliable brand that holds up in the local climate.

BTUs

BTUs are British Thermal Units, which is the method used to measure heat output for stoves and grills. To get a nice brown crust on steaks, you want the highest BTUs for your money.

Burners

Some grills have burners that run right-to-left, and others that run front-to-back. The configuration isn't important, but the number of burners is. The more burners you have, the more control you will have over the heat level. Sometimes you want to crank up the grill for high heat, so four burners will obviously give you more heat than three. Likewise, when you want lower heat (because not everything is blasted on high heat), you have more heat variations when you can adjust the thermostats on four burners instead of three (or two).

Thermometer

You definitely want a thermometer in the lid to check the heat level. It is best to have actual numbers on the thermometer face instead of just colors to indicate the level.

Ease of Service

Buy a brand that is easy to service, as in has great customer service and replacement parts that can be easily purchased at your local hardware superstore or grill showroom. A cheaper brand that isn't supported in your area will cost you way more in the long run if you can't fix a minor issue and the entire unit can't be used. Look online for customer reviews to see which brands have the highest ratings and are good for your area.

just to be sure. The same goes for grills. You can adjust the burners to high, medium, and low levels to control the temperature, and you can move the food off the direct flame to keep it from overcooking on the outside only. Just keep the lid closed—no different from an oven.

Indirect heat has become a lot more popular because people are cooking larger cuts of meat on the grill than they used to. Once you get the hang of it, as I have, you'll never go back to scorching things Flintstones-style.

No matter what kind of heat you use, direct or indirect, you do not have to grease the cooking grate with oil. Usually, the oil drips down onto the burners and you get flames where you don't want them. (The exception is breaded food—an old Italian grilling method that you will love—because a little oil on the grate helps keep the crumbs from sticking.) Just oil the food itself (or use a marinade with a little oil in the recipe) to reduce sticking. One thing for sure: Never spray a hot grate with nonstick oil from an aerosol can!

★ ★ ★ **Grilling No-Nos** ★ ★ ★

—Overcooking your food

—Squishing burgers with the spatula

—Cooking with the lid open

—Using lighter fluid

—Allowing children near the grill

RAW VS. READY

One final reminder about handling raw meat since it will go on a little trip from your fridge to your backyard. Remember that you have to keep raw meat separate from everything else—including your other food, especially veggies—until it's cooked. Be sure to thoroughly clean all counter surfaces that have come in contact with raw meat, and wash your hands in hot, soapy water for at least twenty seconds (about as long as it take you to sing "Happy Birthday" to yourself *twice*).

Also, don't use the same plates that you used to carry the raw meat out to the grill to pile it on after it's cooked. You can use two separate plates, or line one plate with waxed paper, put the raw meat on top, then just throw the paper away so the plate underneath is clean and ready to transport the cooked meat. Same goes for utensils. Once the food is on the grill, you should wash the tongs that handled the raw food before using them again to turn the cooked food.

Now that you know everything about your outdoor kitchen, let's get some food on that grill!

CHAPTER 2

Antipasti (Appetizers)

La cucina piccola fa la casa grande.
Literally: "A small kitchen makes the house big."
What it means: "The best things in life are free."

The key to starting any party—or even any meal for Italians!—is the first course, the *antipasti,* which literally means "before the meal." It's beyond important because it's how you greet your guests, how you show you've been preparing for them and prepping for their arrival with love. It sets the tone for the entire event, both in mood and appetite.

While some people serve hors d'oeuvres on individual china plates in the dining room, Italians prefer to put out big platters of *antipasti* to keep people moving around, walking, talking, drinking, and socializing—especially in the warm summer months when we can be outside. We typically put the antipasti on the bar or tables near the grill so everyone can talk to whomever is cooking the food, and no one is left out or off to the side. So you can see why I don't mind grilling. At our house, it's not a thankless, sweaty job in the corner; it's more like a master-of-ceremonies position!

To tell you the truth, I more than don't mind. I really love doing the actual grilling myself. No joke, I was just outside last night at two in the morning with Joe grilling up some burgers. The women in my family are proud that we can work the grill as well as the guys can. My very first grill was actually my bridal shower present from my mother-in-law!

Formaggio Is for Lovers ✳ ✳ ✳

Italian cheese is no joke. In fact, they take it so seriously in Italy that the Ministry of Agriculture and Forests decides—based on specific ingredient and quality standards—which cheeses from which regions can be labeled as "official." These cheeses are considered so important to the culture of Italy that they are given "protected" status by the government.

Buying imported Italian cheese is like buying imported Italian fashion. Sometimes you just gotta have it and spend the money, but other times, a knockoff is just as good. Don't feel like you always have to drive across town and pay twenty-five dollars per pound for imported Italian cheese. I'd go authentic when the cheese will be eaten on its own, like on a meat-and-cheese platter, but when it will be added to an already strongly flavored dish, American-made equivalents will do just fine. There are wonderful cheeses from Wisconsin and California. To keep the cost of cooking down, I list "Parmesan" in these recipes, but feel free to substitute with Parmigiano-Reggiano if you like.

Here are the most popular cheeses that are easily available in America, that taste amazing, and that you'll find over and over in my recipes:

Asiago

A white cheese with small holes, asiago is a smooth, mild cheese with a slight tang (it gets tangier the more it ages). It is a good substitute for Parmesan cheese.

Burrata

Named for the Italian word for "buttered," burrata is a hollow pocket of soft cheese that resembles fresh buffalo mozzarella on the outside, but has a creamy, curdy cheese that resembles ricotta on the inside. Created in Puglia—the "heel" of Italy—to use up the "extra bits" left behind from making other cheese, burrata is delicious all by itself, but is also great in salads, on pizza, and even as dessert. Just drizzle some honey and put some nuts on it for a very fast and yummy way to end dinner.

Fontina Valle d'Aosta

One of the all-time great Italian cheeses. A light yellow, creamy cheese, fontina is mild tasting with an earthy, slightly nutty taste. You can find domestic "fontina" cheeses, which are also really good.

Gorgonzola

A semisoft, creamy blue cheese, Gorgonzola has a strong aroma and taste but a sweet aftertaste. Italian Gorgonzola comes in two varieties: Dolce is smooth and creamy, and piccante is firm and crumbly. If you are given a choice, buy the kind that suits the recipe at hand. For example, for a salad or pizza, choose piccante because it crumbles best. For most cooking, the American Gorgonzola, which strikes a middle ground between the two Italian varieties, is perfect.

Mozzarella

A bright-white cheese with a smooth, wet, silky texture, mozzarella has a very mild, milky flavor. When I want a treat, I use fresh mozzarella, which is usually shaped in balls and packed in water. When the balls are small, they are called baby bocconcini (pronounced bok-on-CHEE-nee, Italian for "little mouthfuls") or ciliegine (chee-LAY-gee-nie, meaning "little cherries"). The firmer supermarket "pizza-style" mozzarella is fine, too, and it melts beautifully.

Parmigiano-Reggiano

The great-grandfather of the American version we call Parmesan (which has two-thirds more salt than its Italian ancestor) and considered "the king of cheeses" in Italy, Parmigiano-Reggiano is a hard, crumbly, light-yellow cheese with a sharp nutty and fruity taste. This is one of the protected cheeses of Italy; you can't call cheese "Parmigiano-Reggiano" unless it is made in the designated area around Parma. This is one reason why it is more expensive, but worth it.

Pecorino Romano

A white cheese with a straw-yellow tinge, Pecorino Romano is a bold, peppery, nutty cheese that grates beautifully. It is made from sheep's milk and is a lot sharper than "Parm."

Provolone

Most often served in America in slices, provolone is a semihard-but-smooth white cheese with a mild, smoky flavor. (Aged provolone can get very sharp tasting and crumbly, though.)

Ricotta

It's technically not a cheese, but a dairy product made from the whey left over from cheese. Ricotta means "recooked," which is what happens to the whey to firm it up. Ricotta is white, soft, creamy, and slightly sweet.

No matter what you're making for each course, make sure that you're good and prepped. Have all the ingredients you need collected, and cleaned, chopped, diced, shredded, and ready to be added to your dish *before* you start cooking it, especially since your "oven" is farther away from your refrigerator or sink than you're used to. There's nothing worse than scrambling to peel garlic while your steak shrinks into a charred hockey puck. You can't be everyplace at once, so have all you need right next to you at the grill.

✳ ✳ ✳ Teresa's Tips for Great Grilling ✳ ✳ ✳

—Have an extra gas tank on hand—but not stored near the grill—in case you run out mid-sear.

—Always let the grill preheat for between ten and fifteen minutes before you start cooking.

—Never leave a lit grill completely unattended, especially around children.

—Don't let your kids near the grill, period.

—Don't rush. *Nice and slow, nice and low* is better than *hot and burned.*

—Relax! It's definitely not a good idea to get ripped while you're roasting—it's dangerous for you and the food—but a glass of wine or a cold beer while you're basting is almost an Italian tradition.

Kale and Pancetta Bruschetta

Makes 8 servings

Most Americans don't regularly grill bread; they reserve the grate for meat and the occasional veggie. But toasted bread was originally made crispy over open flames, not in a little metal box. In fact, bruschetta got its name from the fact that it's supposed to be cooked on a grill. If you've never made it this way—and even if you have—you are in for a treat. My version marries bold kale with smooth pancetta. This recipe works with broccoli rabe standing in for the kale, too.

Kale:

2 pounds kale, either dark green curly or the "Tuscan" variety

⅓ cup diced (¼-inch cubes) pancetta

1 tablespoon olive oil

1 small onion, chopped

2 garlic cloves, minced

½ teaspoon red pepper flakes

Salt

2 plum (Roma) tomatoes, seeded and cut into ½-inch dice

Bruschetta:

1 loaf crusty Italian bread, cut into about 24 (¼-inch-thick) slices

Extra-virgin olive oil

Freshly grated Parmesan cheese, for serving

1. To cook the kale: Tear the kale leaves from the thick stems; discard the stems. A few at a time, stack the leaves and cut crosswise into strips about ½ inch thick. Wash the strips well in a large sink of cold water (kale is gritty). Lift up the strips and transfer to a colander, leaving any grit behind in the sink. Do not dry the kale.

2. Heat the pancetta and oil together in a large skillet over medium heat, stirring often, until the pancetta is crisp and browned, about 8 minutes. Using a slotted spoon, transfer the pancetta to paper towels, leaving the fat in the pan.

3. Add the onion to the skillet and cook over medium heat, stirring occasionally, until softened, about 3 minutes. Stir in the garlic and cook until fragrant, about 1 minute. In two or three additions, stir in the kale, letting the first addition wilt before adding more. Return the pancetta to the skillet. Stir in the red pepper flakes and season with salt. Cover and cook, stirring occasionally, until the kale is very tender, adding a few tablespoons of water if the liquid cooks away, about 20 minutes. During the last 5 minutes, stir in the tomatoes. Reduce the heat to very low and cover to keep warm.

4. Meanwhile, preheat the grill for direct cooking over medium heat (400°F).

5. To make the bruschetta: Brush the bread slices on both sides with the oil. Place on the cooking grate and close the grill lid. Cook, turning as needed, until toasted, about 2 minutes. Remove the bread slices from the grill.

6. Spoon the kale mixture on the bread slices. Sprinkle with the Parmesan and serve hot.

✳ ✳ ✳ Bruschetta vs. Crostini ✳ ✳ ✳

While both are slices of toasted bread topped with cheese, vegetables, or meat, there is a difference between *bruschetta* and *crostini*. Bruschetta, from the Italian *bruscare*, which means to "roast over coals," is made with large slices of bread, brushed with olive oil and toasted on a grill over open flames (like we're doing here). Sometimes the toasted bread is rubbed with garlic before topping. Crostini or "little toasts" in Italian, are cut from a thinner loaf of bread (such as a baguette), and they can be baked or grilled until they are crisp and crunchy.

Whichever one you're serving, be sure to get started with a loaf that doesn't have too many holes in it, or your yummy topping will fall through.

✳ ✳ ✳   Toast Toppings   ✳ ✳ ✳

Now that you know the fundamentals of making bruschetta and crostini, you can personalize them in your own style. Here are some of my favorite toppings:

—Homemade Pesto (page 161)

—Store-bought sun-dried tomato pesto

—Olivada (page 42)

—Quartered figs (raw or grilled) and Gorgonzola

—Canned tuna (preferably imported Italian in olive oil), mashed with capers, lemon juice, and red onion

—Prosciutto and roasted red peppers

—Italian sausage, chopped basil, and fontina

—Grilled Marinated Portobello Mushrooms (page 48), sliced

—Ripe plum (Roma) tomatoes finely chopped with olive oil, basil, and garlic

—Artichoke hearts, chopped, mixed with lemon juice, cayenne pepper, and asiago cheese

—Fresh mozzarella marinated overnight in olive oil with garlic and fresh herbs

You can even make tiny toasts for dessert:

—Mascarpone and sliced fresh peaches, nectarines, or cherries

—Nutella and banana slices

—Sliced strawberries marinated in Grand Marnier

—Dark chocolate sprinkled with coarse sea salt

Tuscan White Bean Crostini

Makes 16 slices of crostini, 6 to 8 servings

In Italy, we love our beans. We serve them for appetizers (just like this spread), in salads, and even in sweet bean cakes! If they're not part of your weekly diet, you should change that now. You can begin with this starter. This spread can be made in a flash with things you probably have in the kitchen anyway. You can also serve it with any kind of cracker, or even as a dip for veggies (red bell pepper strips are especially tasty).

Bean Spread:

1 (15.5-ounce) can white kidney beans (cannellini), drained and rinsed

2 tablespoons chopped fresh basil or flat-leaf parsley, plus more for serving

1 tablespoon fresh lemon juice

2 garlic cloves, minced

¼ teaspoon red pepper flakes

¼ cup extra-virgin olive oil, plus more for drizzling

Salt

Crostini:

16 (¼-inch-thick) slices baguette

Extra-virgin olive oil

1. To make the bean spread: Purée the beans, basil, lemon juice, garlic, and red pepper flakes in a food processor. With the machine running, add the oil. Season with salt to taste. Transfer to a bowl. (The bean spread can be covered and refrigerated for up to 3 days.)

2. Meanwhile, preheat the grill for direct cooking over medium heat (400°F).

3. To make the crostini: Brush the bread slices on both sides with the oil. Place the bread slices on the cooking grate and close the grill lid. Cook, turning as needed, until toasted, about 2 minutes. Remove the bread slices from the grill.

4. Spread about 1 tablespoon of the bean spread on each crostini. Drizzle with additional oil, sprinkle with the additional basil, and serve.

Olivada

Makes about 1¼ cups, 8 servings

You know by now that the Giudices love (in no particular order) garlic, olive oil, red pepper flakes, olives, anchovies, and fresh herbs. Olivada, a black olive spread, has them all! It's one of those things that you should make according to your taste with as much pepper, garlic, or anchovies as you like (or love!). Stashed in the refrigerator, it keeps for a few weeks, ready to be spread on bruschetta, spooned onto tomatoes for a quick salad, stirred into vinaigrette to perk up dressing, or tossed with a little spaghetti.

2 garlic cloves, crushed under the flat side of a knife and peeled

4 anchovy fillets in olive oil, drained and coarsely chopped

2 teaspoons finely chopped fresh rosemary or 1 tablespoon finely chopped fresh basil

¼ teaspoon red pepper flakes, or more to taste

2 cups pitted Kalamata or green olives, or 1 cup of each

⅓ cup extra-virgin olive oil, plus more for storage

1. In a food processor, with the machine running, drop the garlic through the feed tube to mince it. Add the anchovies, rosemary, and red pepper flakes and pulse the machine a few times until they are minced. Add the olives and pulse until very finely chopped. With the machine running, gradually add the oil to make a thick paste. (Or, in a blender, working in batches, process all of the ingredients together, scraping down the sides of the container as needed.)

2. Transfer the olivada to a covered container and smooth the top. Serve at room temperature. (To store, pour a thin layer of oil over the top of the olivada and refrigerate for up to 1 month. Before serving, remove the olivada from the refrigerator, stir in the top layer of oil, and let stand at room temperature for 1 hour.)

✳ ✳ ✳ As Good as Bread ✳ ✳ ✳

It's no secret that Italians love their bread, but for us bread is chewy, hearty, and crispy—not the giant doughy loaves of white stuff they call "Italian bread" in the United States. We often serve bread in small portions—in the form of bruschetta, grissini (breadsticks or crostini)—and that's much healthier, and I think, much more delicious.

A lot of Italian proverbs have to do with bread. For instance, we say *pan di sudore, miglior sapore,* which translates to "bread that comes out of sweat tastes better." It's true too. You appreciate most what you work hardest for. Instead of saying "to call a spade a spade," we say *pane al pane, vino al vino,* or "bread is bread, wine is wine." We don't say someone or something is as "good as gold." Instead, we say *e buono come il pane* or "it's as good as bread." And my favorite, because it's true, is *pan e pagn ai nu fai mai dagn,* "you can never have too much bread or clothes."

Grilled Ciambotta

Makes about 1 quart, 12 servings

If I can win a cook-off in a trailer park using tiny RV burners to make my family's famous ciambotta, you can definitely wow your friends on a proper grill. This quick and easy eggplant appetizer can be served alone, with bread, or on top of bruschetta or crostini.

⅓ cup extra-virgin olive oil

4 garlic cloves, crushed under the flat side of a knife and peeled

1 large eggplant, cut into ½-inch-thick rounds

4 plum (Roma) tomatoes, cut in halfs lengthwise

2 tablespoons chopped fresh basil or 1 tablespoon chopped fresh oregano, plus more for serving

¼ teaspoon red pepper flakes

Salt

1. Heat the oil and garlic together in a small saucepan over medium heat until small bubbles form around the garlic, about 3 minutes. Remove from the heat and let stand for about 15 minutes. Using a fork, remove and reserve the garlic.

2. Preheat the grill for direct cooking over medium heat (400°F).

3. Arrange the eggplant on a large baking sheet and brush both sides with the garlic oil. Place the eggplant directly on the cooking grate, and close the grill lid. Cook the eggplant until the undersides are golden brown and seared with grill marks, about 5 minutes. Flip the eggplant and continue cooking, with the lid closed, until the other side is golden brown and the eggplant is tender, about 5 minutes more. Remove the eggplant from the grill.

4. Brush the tomatoes all over with the remaining garlic oil. Place the tomatoes, cut-side down, on the cooking grate and close the grill lid. Cook until seared with grill marks, about 5 minutes. Flip the tomatoes over and cook, with the lid closed, until the peel is seared and splitting, about 3 minutes. Remove the tomatoes from the grill.

5. Pulse the eggplant, tomatoes, reserved garlic, any remaining garlic oil, basil, and red pepper flakes in a food processor to make a chunky purée. (Or put all of the ingredients in a large bowl and mash with a potato masher.) Transfer to a medium bowl and let cool.

6. Cover and refrigerate until chilled, at least 2 hours and up to 2 days. Sprinkle with the additional basil and serve chilled or at room temperature.

* * * Italian Ingredient(e)s * * *

When I was a kid, you could only get a lot of the ingredients for our traditional kind of cooking at little, local Italian grocery stores. Thankfully, the popularity of Italian cooking and the evolution of specialty grocery chains like Trader Joe's and Whole Foods have changed that. You can now get baccalà and bocconcini, prosciutto and pancetta, borlotti beans, and reasonably priced, amazing, imported olive oil at national chains, along with great veal chops, fresh basil, and wonderful salami. *Viva L'Italia!*

Mini-Peppers with Sausage-Ricotta Stuffing

Makes 16

Serve as part of a bigger antipasto platter so your guests can balance these stuffed peppers with a few not-so-rich items like olive or pickled veggies. You'll find the miniature peppers in lots of supermarkets. Choose ones "a little larger than bite" size.

Stuffing

1 tablespoon extra-virgin olive oil
1 medium onion, finely chopped
1 garlic clove, finely chopped
6 ounces sweet turkey sausage, casings removed (about 2 links)
½ cup ricotta cheese
¼ cup Italian-seasoned dry bread crumbs
1 large egg, beaten
1 tablespoon fresh flat-leaf parsley, finely chopped
¼ teaspoon salt
⅛ teaspoon freshly ground black pepper

Peppers

Extra-virgin olive oil, for the pan and serving
16 miniature red, yellow, green, and orange bell peppers
Fresh flat-leaf parsley, finely chopped, for serving

1. Heat the oil in a medium skillet over medium heat. Add the onion and cook, stirring occasionally, until softened, about 3 minutes. Add the garlic and cook until fragrant, about 1 minute more. Add the sausage and cook, breaking up the sausage with the side of a wooden spoon, until it loses its raw look, about 8 minutes. Transfer to a bowl and let cool completely. Stir in the ricotta cheese, bread crumbs, egg, parsley, salt, and pepper.

2. Lightly oil a 13 x 9-inch metal or disposable aluminum foil roasting pan. Cut each pepper in half lengthwise, keeping the stem intact. Using a small spoon, scoop out and discard the seeds and ribs. Stuff each pepper with the ricotta mixture. Arrange the peppers, stuffed sides up, in the pan. Drizzle with the oil. Pour ½ cup of hot water into the pan.

3. Prepare the grill for indirect cooking with medium heat (400°F).

4. Place the pan on the grill over the not-yet-ignited burner(s). Close the lid and cook until the topping is lightly browned and the peppers are tender, 30 to 40 minutes. Remove from the grill.

5. Drizzle with the oil and sprinkle with the parsley. Serve warm or cooled to room temperature.

Grilled Marinated Portobello Mushrooms

Makes 4 servings, more if part of an antipasti platter

There are so many ways you can present these delicious mushrooms. Serve the mushrooms whole, warm, or at room temperature with fresh green salad as a first course. Cut them into wedges and serve with toothpicks as part of an antipasti platter. Tie a string around two of them and use as a bikini top. OK, maybe not that last one, but you can definitely finish them off with your favorite fresh herbs, alone or in a tasty combination.

2 tablespoons balsamic vinegar

2 garlic cloves, minced

¼ teaspoon salt

¼ teaspoon freshly ground black pepper

⅓ cup extra-virgin olive oil

4 (4-inch) portobello mushroom caps

1 tablespoon finely chopped fresh basil, oregano, or parsley, or 2 teaspoons finely chopped fresh thyme or sage, *optional*

1. Whisk the vinegar, garlic, salt, and pepper together in a small bowl. Gradually whisk in the oil. Pour into a shallow glass or ceramic baking dish. Add the mushrooms and turn to coat both sides. Let stand at room temperature, turning occasionally, for about 30 minutes.

2. Preheat the grill for direct cooking over medium heat (400°F).

3. Remove the mushrooms from the baking dish, reserving any marinade. Place the mushrooms on the cooking grate, gill sides up, and close the grill lid. Cook until the undersides are seared with grill marks, about 3 minutes. Flip the mushrooms and continue cooking, with the lid closed until tender and juicy, 3 to 4 minutes more. Transfer the mushrooms to a serving platter. Let cool for 10 minutes.

4. Sprinkle with the herbs and drizzle with the reserved marinade. Serve warm or at room temperature.

CHAPTER 3

Pizza

Quel che non ammazza, ingrassa.

Literally: "What won't kill you, will feed (fatten) you."

What it means: "What doesn't kill you makes you stronger."

Along with an assortment of meats and cheeses and the special grilled antipasti dishes we always serve, one of the most popular first courses for Italians is pizza. Most people don't think you can cook a pizza on the grill, but it's really no different than cooking it on a flat rack in your oven. Perfect pizzas require a lot of heat (by oven standards, anyway), so it's only natural in a hot country to want to cook them outside. Some people, like Joe's parents, have permanent pizza ovens built in their backyards, but the rest of us manage just fine on the regular grill.

Even though we eat them as a first course, you could easily make any of these pizzas for your main entrée. And once you get the hang of the dough and the process, you can create your own signature pies by making them with your favorite toppings.

PIZZA ON THE GRILL

Cooking pizza on the grill is one of my family's favorite things to do. The key is to be super-organized. Have all of the toppings ready to go—sliced, shredded, and precooked, as needed. You can even partially grill the pizza dough to get it ready for the toppings.

When grilling pizza, the dough goes right on the cooking grate, so you don't need a baking stone, as you would in an oven. You will see grilling pizza stones for sale, but they don't work that well. To slide the pizza dough onto the cooking grate without ripping or squishing it, you can either use a wooden baker's peel (one of those large paddle/shovel-looking things) or just use a large rimless baking sheet (or the bottom of a turned-over regular baking sheet). We make pizza a lot, so we have a paddle. You can get one for less than fifteen dollars at your local discount supercenter.

Medium Heat

The big secret to grilling pizza is to use "medium heat" that's about 400°F. If the heat is too high, the dough will burn. I promise you, the dough is going to brown at 400°F! You have much more control over the process if the heat isn't blasting. So start by preheating the grill to that sweet spot of 400°F.

The Pizza Process

Each ball of my Pronto Presto Pizza Dough (see page 55) will make a twelve-inch pizza. Here's what to do once you've made it: Spread the dough on a floured work surface and flatten it with your hands into a thick round. From this point, it is easy to roll, stretch, and/or pull the dough into a twelve-inch round. If the dough retracts, just cover it with a damp towel and let it relax for about five minutes, then proceed. Be sure that you have enough flour under the dough that it doesn't stick.

Now sprinkle and spread a couple of tablespoons of flour onto the baker's peel (or rimless or upturned baking sheet). It should be in a very thin layer. Transfer the dough round to the peel and reshape it as needed. Give the peel a gentle shake to be sure that there is enough flour under the dough that it slides easily, and add more if needed.

Bring the dough to the grill. Using long tongs, dip a wad of paper towels in olive oil and lightly but thoroughly wipe the cooking grate to grease it. (Don't let the oil drip onto the burners, or you'll have some scary flare-ups!) Slide the dough round from the peel right onto the grate. Close the grill lid. Cook until the underside of the dough round is set and browned, three to five minutes. Brush the top of the dough with a little oil. Using a wide spatula, flip the dough over. Brush off any flour from the top of the dough. At this point, quickly add your toppings.

Cover the grill again and cook until the bottom of the pizza is very toasty and the cheese on the topping is melted, three to five minutes more.

Use the baker's peel and spatula to remove the pizza from the grill. Let it stand for a minute, and then cut into wedges and serve hot. Return to the kitchen and repeat with the remaining dough and topping ingredients.

Too Much on Top

Speaking of ingredients, you can put just about anything on pizza. But, you do have to be careful not to overload the dough, or your pizza will end up looking like a boob-job gone bad—sad and saggy. Also, there are some popular ingredients that should be cooked (grilled or sautéed) in advance: pork or turkey sausage and ground meat, most vegetables (they give off juices as they cook that will make the dough wet and soggy), and bacon and pancetta. Once you get to the grilling stage, you are really just warming up the toppings on the pizza, and not actually cooking them.

Par-cooking

When you have a crowd, it helps to have the dough partially cooked so that all you need to do is top, heat, and eat. To pre-cook the dough (or par-cook it as they say in those fancy culinary schools), roll it out, and grill until each side is just set and barely browned, about 3 minutes per side. When you are ready to serve, return the dough to the preheated grill and cook to warm the underside, about 1 minute. Turn the dough over, add the toppings, and grill until the other side is toasted and the toppings are hot and melted, 3 to 5 minutes more.

THE DOUGH AND THE SAUCE

A pizza basically has three components: the dough, the sauce, and the toppings. Toppings can be as simple as grated cheese thrown on top or as elegant as pre-cooked sautéed gourmet meat-and-vegetable combinations. You can pretty much put anything on a pizza—just make sure the flavors go together! But you have to have a good start.

Here are my homemade recipes for pizza dough and red sauce. Both are quick, easy, inexpensive, and will convince you (hopefully!) to never buy store-bought, preservative-filled versions again.

Pronto Presto Pizza Dough

Makes enough dough for 2 (12-inch) pizzas

This is super-fast and easy to make in a standing mixer, but you can also go it old school and mix it by hand. I give you directions for both.

2²/3 cups bread flour, as needed, divided

2 tablespoons extra-virgin olive oil

1 (¹/4-ounce) package instant or quick-rise yeast (2¹/4 teaspoons)

1 teaspoon salt

1 cup hot tap water (not hotter than 130°F)

1. Mix 1¹/4 cups of flour, the oil, yeast, and salt in the bowl of a heavy-duty standing mixer. Add the hot water. Attach the bowl to the mixer and fit it with the paddle attachment. Mix on low speed until the batter is elastic, about 4 minutes. (To make by hand, stir all of the ingredients together in a large bowl with a wooden spoon for about 100 strokes.) Cover with a towel and let stand for 10 minutes.

2. Mix in enough of the remaining flour to make a dough that cleans the sides of the bowl. Remove the paddle attachment and attach the dough hook. Knead on medium speed until the dough is smooth and supple, about 4 minutes. (To continue by hand, stir in enough of the remaining flour to make a dough that is too stiff to stir. Scrape out onto a floured work surface. Knead, adding more flour as needed, to make a soft, tacky dough, about 8 minutes.)

3. Shape the dough into a ball. Transfer to a large bowl (no need to oil the bowl), and cover with a damp towel. Let stand in a warm, draft-free place until the dough doubles in volume, about 30 minutes.

4. Cut the dough in half and shape each half into a ball. Use immediately. (Or, place the dough balls in a well-oiled baking dish just large enough to hold the balls. Turn the balls to coat well with oil. Cover tightly with plastic wrap, and refrigerate for up to 24 hours. Remove from the refrigerator 1 hour before using.)

"The Quickie" Tomato Sauce

Makes about 3½ cups

There is no need to buy store-bought all-purpose *salsa al pomodoro* when you can make it as quickly as this from scratch. The Quickie is a wonderful base not just for pizza, but also for pasta, juicy meat, or even just as a dip for bread or breadsticks. You can add other ingredients, like sausage or red pepper flakes, to this versatile sauce.

1 tablespoon extra-virgin olive oil

1 (28-ounce) can imported whole Italian plum tomatoes, broken up with their juices

¼ cup tomato paste

2 tablespoons chopped fresh basil

2 garlic cloves, minced, *optional*

1 medium onion, finely chopped, *optional*

1. Heat the oil in a large saucepan over medium heat, adding garlic or onion, see variation below. Add the tomatoes and their juices and the tomato paste. Bring just to a boil.

2. Reduce the heat to medium-low and add the basil. Simmer to blend the flavors, about 10 minutes.

"The Quickie" Tomato Sauce with Garlic: Heat garlic cloves, minced, with the oil in the saucepan over medium heat until the garlic is softened and fragrant, about 2 minutes. Proceed as directed.

"The Quickie" Tomato Sauce with Onion: Heat the oil in a large saucepan over medium heat. Add onion, finely chopped, and cook, stirring occasionally, until the onion is softened, about 3 minutes. Proceed as directed.

Zucchini and Red Onion Pizza

Makes one 12-inch pizza

This amazing vegetarian pizza proves that you don't have to put meat on a pizza for it to be good. People have been grilling zucchini for years, so don't be afraid that it will fall through the grate. Just be sure to place the strips perpendicular to the cooking grate.

1 medium zucchini, cut lengthwise into ¼-inch-thick strips

½ small red onion, cut into thin half-moons

1 tablespoon extra-virgin olive oil, plus more for brushing

1 tablespoon balsamic vinegar

Salt and freshly ground black pepper

1 ball Pronto Presto Pizza Dough (page 55)

Flour, for rolling out the dough

½ cup "The Quickie" Tomato Sauce with Garlic (facing page)

¼ cup freshly grated Pecorino Romano cheese

1. Preheat the grill for direct cooking over medium heat (400°F).

2. Toss the zucchini, onion, olive oil, and vinegar in a medium bowl and season with salt and pepper. Place the zucchini strips on the cooking grate and close the grill lid. Cook until the undersides are seared with grill marks, about 2 minutes. Flip the zucchini and cook, with the lid closed, until the other sides are seared, about 2 minutes more. Remove the zucchini strips from the grill and cut into 2-inch pieces.

3. On a lightly floured work surface, roll, pull, and stretch the dough into a 12-inch round. Transfer to a lightly floured baker's peel (or rimless baking sheet) and reshape as needed.

4. Lightly oil the cooking grate. Slide the dough from the peel onto the grate and close the grill lid. Cook until the underside is browned with grill marks, 3 to 5 minutes. Lightly brush the top of the dough with oil. Flip the dough over and brush off any flour. Spread the tomato sauce on the dough, leaving a ¾-inch border. Top with the zucchini and onion and sprinkle with the Romano cheese. Close the lid and continue cooking until the underside is browned, 3 to 5 minutes. Remove the pizza from the grill, and let it stand 1 to 2 minutes, then cut into wedges and serve.

White Pizza

Makes one 12-inch pizza

True white pizza has extra cheese and uses basil as its main seasoning. "Untrue" white pizza uses American-invented, artery-clogging Alfredo sauce instead of tomato sauce. Do your heart, stomach, and taste buds a favor and go with the former. Here's a light, delicious version.

¼ cup ricotta cheese

1 teaspoon extra-virgin olive oil, plus more for brushing

1 garlic clove, minced

1 ball Pronto Presto Pizza Dough (page 55)

Flour, for rolling out the dough

4 ounces fresh mozzarella, thinly sliced

2 tablespoon coarsely chopped fresh basil

1. Mix the ricotta, oil, and garlic together in a small bowl. Let stand at room temperature for about 30 minutes.

2. Preheat the grill for direct cooking over medium heat (400°F).

3. Roll, pull, and stretch the dough on a lightly floured work surface into a 12-inch round. Transfer to a lightly floured baker's peel (or a rimless baking sheet) and reshape as needed.

4. Lightly oil the cooking grate. Slide the dough from the peel onto the grate and close the grill lid. Cook until the underside is browned, 3 to 5 minutes. Lightly brush the top of the dough with oil. Flip the dough over and brush off any flour. Spread the ricotta mixture on the dough, leaving a ¾-inch border. Top with the mozzarella. Close the lid and continue cooking until the underside is browned, 3 to 5 minutes. Remove the pizza from the grill, and let it stand 1 to 2 minutes. Sprinkle the pizza with the basil, cut into wedges, and serve.

✳ ✳ ✳ **Pizza Bianca** ✳ ✳ ✳

Pizza is one of the world's oldest prepared foods—flatbread with toppings has been around since biblical times. But originally all pizza was "white" (without tomato sauce) because for centuries people, especially in Europe, thought that tomatoes were poisonous. Turns out the lead in everyone's pewter plates and flatware would leach into foods high in acids, like tomatoes, and people would die of lead poisoning. It was years before they would figure out that their plates—not the ripe, red fruits—were the problem.

Fig, Prosciutto, and Gorgonzola Pizza

Makes one 12-inch pizza

I'm a huge fig fan, especially when paired with salty prosciutto and crumbled Gorgonzola. You can serve this incredible pizza an as appetizer, a main course, or even as a savory dessert.

1 ball of Pronto Presto Pizza Dough (page 55)
Flour, for rolling out the dough
8 very thin slices of prosciutto
8 ripe figs, stemmed and quartered
1 cup (5 ounces) crumbled Gorgonzola cheese
Extra-virgin olive oil

1. Preheat the grill for direct cooking over medium heat (400°F).

2. Roll, pull, and stretch the dough on a lightly floured work surface into a 12-inch round. Transfer to a lightly floured baker's peel (or a rimless baking sheet) and reshape as needed.

3. Lightly oil the cooking grate. Slide the dough from the peel onto the grate and close the grill lid. Cook until the underside is browned, 3 to 5 minutes. Lightly brush the top of the dough with oil. Flip the dough over and brush off any flour. Arrange the prosciutto and figs evenly over the dough, then sprinkle with the Gorgonzola. Close the lid and continue cooking until the underside is browned, 3 to 5 minutes. Remove the pizza from the grill, and let it stand 1 to 2 minutes. Drizzle with olive oil, cut into wedges, and serve.

CHAPTER 4

Insalate e Minestre (Salads and Soups)

The way we say "take it or leave it" in Italy—
usually with a shrug—is
a mangiar questa minestra o saltar questa fincestra,
which means "either eat this soup or
jump out this window."

I know there are people who say you can grill anything, even watermelon, but I think that's a little insane. (I've actually tasted grilled watermelon, but it's too watery to do anything but get hot. You know what's not so refreshing on a hot day? Hot watermelon.) Not all food is meant for the grill, and if you plan on grilling all of your courses you'll end up spending all day cooking and not interacting with your guests.

For first courses and lighter entrées, I prefer quickly grilling key ingredients and then adding them to the rest of the nongrilled dish to make something more like magic. For instance, arugula salad with figs is delicious. Grill the figs first, though, and it becomes divine. Macaroni salad is yummy, until you add grill-roasted red peppers, and then it becomes art.

I'm also going to give you some soups and cold salads that don't need to go anywhere near your grill so you can enjoy your own party. And you can easily make any of these recipes ahead of time, so when people start arriving, you can just pull them out of the refrigerator and dig in.

Of course, all my recipes celebrate the fruits of the summer season. There is nothing like fresh strawberries, just-picked basil, or locally grown tomatoes. In fact, those three favorites are some of the easiest plants to grow at home, yourself. If you've never done it, it's well worth the time and will save you lots of money! I have fresh basil year round: in my garden in the summer and in pots inside in the winter. My girls love to grow strawberries (although most only manage to make it from the vine directly into their mouths!). And tomatoes . . . the taste difference alone between those grown at home or on a small farm and those that are commercially grown should be enough to convince anyone to start staking out a small garden plot.

---

* * * **Re-seasoning Salads** * * *

Starchy salads—like potato and macaroni—soak up their dressings as they sit in the refrigerator, and the flavors change. Something that may have been perfectly seasoned a few hours before may taste bland now. So always re-season these salads as needed with a splash of vinegar or oil and a sprinkle of salt and pepper. If you are taking them to a picnic or cookout, make some extra dressing and bring it along for re-seasoning.

WHICH VINEGAR?

Like peanut butter to jelly, olive oil needs its friend vinegar to make Italian summer dressings and marinades perfect. Which vinegar—balsamic, white wine, or red wine—should you always have on hand? The answer is all of them, since they all have different tastes and colors and uses.

Balsamic is amazingly delicious, especially on salad, but its slightly sweet flavor and dark color isn't right for everything. White wine vinegar is a little on the expensive side, but a little goes a long way; it's great for poultry and fish dishes, or even drizzled on a sandwich. And red wine vinegar is a staple for anything to do with red meat. I use it a lot in my marinades for red meat because the acid helps the marinade penetrate into the meat better.

JUST ADD CHICKEN

Salads and soups in Italy are starter courses, but you can add protein, such as grilled chicken, to any of the following recipes and have a wonderfully filling main entrée.

✳ ✳ ✳ Hydroponic Blah ✳ ✳ ✳

t's not your imagination: supermarket tomatoes, even in season, don't taste as good as they did thirty years ago. My mom insisted it was true, so I looked it up and as always, she was right. To get the best crop possible, today's mass-produced tomatoes have been bred specifically for looks and long transportation times. Taste? Well, that didn't seem to crossover very well. Add to that the fact that they are picked a month before they're ripe, and then stored, shipped, and sometimes even squirted with ethylene gas to artificially make them look "natural," and it's no wonder that they don't taste as good as they do right off the farm. Do what you can to find a farmers' market, or go get a big pot and start planting now!

Grilled Fig and Arugula Salad
with Goat Cheese

Makes 6 servings

Grilling figs brings out their honey-like juices and makes them even sweeter. They are a wonderful complement to the pungent arugula and the sharp and creamy goat cheese. The heat from the grilled figs wilts the arugula and lightly melts the cheese—all the better to bring out their flavor. To give the salad more color, use red grapes if you have green figs, or green grapes if you have the reddish-brown ones.

9 large ripe brown or green figs, stemmed and cut in half lengthwise

¼ cup extra-virgin olive oil, plus more for brushing the figs

4 ounces (about 6 cups) baby or regular arugula leaves

1 cup halved red or green seedless grapes

Salt and freshly ground black pepper

1 cup (4 ounces) crumbled goat cheese

1 lemon, cut into 6 wedges

1. Preheat the grill for direct cooking over medium-high heat (400°F).

2. Lightly brush the figs with olive oil. Place them on the cooking grate and close the grill lid. Cook, flipping once, until seared with grill marks and the juices are bubbling, about 2 minutes per side. Remove the figs from the grill.

3. Toss the baby arugula and grapes with the cup oil. Season with salt and pepper. Divide among six dinner plates. Top each with 3 fig halves and the crumbled goat cheese. Add a lemon wedge to each plate and serve immediately. Pass a peppermill at the table to add pepper to the figs and goat cheese, if desired.

✳ ✳ ✳ Arugula ✳ ✳ ✳

I told you that Italians like it hot, and that even goes for our lettuce! We can't get enough of peppery arugula. I love it in my salads, and some people cook with it, too. Standard arugula is sold at just about every Jersey farm stand during the summer.

Be sure to remove the tough stems and wash the leaves very well in cold water to remove the grit. The best way to dry the leaves without crushing them is with a salad spinner, or you can blot them dry with paper towels.

Baby arugula, which is a little less spicy, can be found in almost every supermarket produce section. Even though baby arugula can be pricey, it takes much less prep time since you don't have to remove the stems—just rinse, spin, and serve.

Iceberg Lettuce Wedge with Gorgonzola and Pancetta Crumbles

Makes 4 to 6 servings

This isn't the steakhouse wedge salad with the super-thick blue cheese dressing, but a somewhat lighter version with an Italian groove. The vinaigrette that has a little kick thanks to garlic and paprika and crumbled Gorgonzola. You can use any kind of blue cheese, really, just as long as it is firm and crumbles well (avoid using creamy kinds of blue cheese). If you are serving to people with big appetites, then serve the lettuce in quarters, but you can also cut the lettuce into six wedges for smaller portions.

Pancetta Crumbles:
4 ounces (1/8-inch thick)
    sliced pancetta
1 tablespoon extra-virgin olive oil

Dressing:
2 tablespoons white or
    red wine vinegar
1 garlic clove, crushed through
    a press
1/2 teaspoon sweet paprika
1/4 teaspoon salt
1/4 teaspoon freshly ground
    black pepper
1/2 cup plus 1 tablespoon
    extra-virgin olive oil
1 1/4 cups (5 ounces) crumbled
    Gorgonzola
1 firm head iceberg lettuce, cored,
    cut into quarters or sixths
1 ripe tomato, seeded and diced

1. To make the pancetta crumbles: In a large skillet, cook the pancetta with the oil over medium heat, turning as needed until crisp and brown, about 6 to 8 minutes. (Don't cook any longer because overcooked pancetta can be tough.) Transfer the pancetta to paper towels to drain. Let cool completely. Coarsely chop the pancetta. Cover and refrigerate until ready to use, up to 2 days.

2. To make the dressing: In a medium bowl, whisk the vinegar, garlic, paprika, salt, and pepper together. Gradually whisk in the oil. Whisk in the Gorgonzola.

3. Place a lettuce wedge, curved-side down, on each of four dinner plates. Spoon equal amounts of the dressing over the lettuce wedges, and sprinkle the tomatoes and pancetta on top. Serve immediately.

Macaroni Salad with Pepperoncini

Makes 8 servings

Every family needs a fantastic macaroni salad that will put the stuff in the deli case to shame. My recipe starts with the basics of elbow macaroni and mayo, but it takes a turn with the veggies. The secret is pepperoncini, sweet Tuscan pickled peppers. Just like many American cooks trick out their pasta salads with dill pickle "juice," I use some of the pepper brine from the jar as an out-of-this-world seasoning.

1 pound (16 ounces) elbow macaroni

2 large red bell peppers, roasted, peeled, and diced (see page 178)

1 cup thawed frozen peas

6 to 8 pepperoncini, coarsely chopped

½ cup finely chopped red onion

½ cup pitted and coarsely chopped olives

2 tablespoons red wine vinegar

2 tablespoons pepperoncini brine from the jar

2/3 cup mayonnaise

1 teaspoon sweet paprika, plus more for garnish

Salt and freshly ground black pepper

1. Bring a large saucepan of salted water to a boil over high heat. Add the macaroni and cook according to the package directions until tender, about 9 minutes. Drain and rinse under cold running water. Drain well and transfer to a large bowl.

2. Add the roasted bell pepper, peas, peperoncini, onion, and olives, and mix well. Sprinkle with the vinegar and peperoncini brine, and mix again. Stir in the mayonnaise and paprika. Season with salt and pepper. Cover and refrigerate for at least 2 hours or up to 2 days.

3. Just before serving, taste the salad and reseason with vinegar, peperoncini brine, salt, and pepper. Sprinkle paprika on top and serve chilled.

Patata Rossa (Red Potato) Salad

Makes 8 servings

Red-skinned potatoes make great potato salad because you get to skip the peeling step. Just scrub the skins well under cold running water before cooking. White-skinned potatoes or Yukon Golds, with their thin peels, also work well here. In this Italian version of potato salad, we skip the mayo and use extra-virgin olive oil and white wine vinegar instead.

3 pounds medium red-skinned potatoes, well scrubbed but unpeeled

¼ cup white wine vinegar

½ teaspoon salt

¼ teaspoon freshly ground black pepper, plus more to taste

¾ cup extra-virgin olive oil

½ cup finely chopped red onion

4 celery ribs, thinly sliced

3 tablespoons finely chopped fresh flat-leaf parsley, basil, or oregano

1. Put the potatoes in a large pot and add enough lightly salted water to cover by 1 inch. Cover tightly and bring to a boil over high heat. Uncover and reduce the heat to medium-low. Cook at a low boil until the potatoes are tender when pierced with the tip of a sharp knife, about 20 minutes. Drain and rinse the potatoes under cold running water. Let stand for about 10 minutes, or until easy to handle.

2. Cut up the warm potatoes into bite-size pieces and transfer to a large bowl. Whisk the vinegar, salt, and pepper together in a medium bowl. Gradually whisk in the oil to make a dressing. Gently stir the dressing into the potatoes, trying not to break up the potatoes. Stir in the red onion, celery, and parsley. Let cool. Cover and refrigerate for at least 2 hours or up to 2 days.

3. When ready to serve, taste the salad and reseason with vinegar, oil, salt, and pepper. Serve chilled or at room temperature.

Mama's Frutti di Mare Seafood Salad

Makes 12 servings

This is traditionally one of the fish dishes that we serve on Christmas Eve, but it's such a great summer recipe that my mom has started to make it at our Shore house. Every time she does, everyone goes nuts and asks for the recipe. So here it is! It makes *a lot*, but it keeps well. I love octopus, but you can substitute with scallops or more shrimp if you like. Leave plenty of time to cook the octopus and scungilli because you can never really tell how long it will take (allow at least 1½ hours for each, but don't be surprised it they take an hour more), and it's best to make them at the same time in separate pots. Because of the time factor, take my advice and make this the day before serving so you aren't rushed and the salad can marinate. My mom doesn't, but feel free to add freshly ground black pepper or red pepper flakes for an extra kick.

Special Equipment:
Corks from 2 wine bottles

1 (3-pound) fresh or thawed frozen octopus
2 pounds fresh or thawed frozen scungilli, cleaned
Salt
2 pounds (31 to 36 count) medium shrimp, peeled and deveined
½ cup fresh lemon juice, plus more for serving
3 garlic cloves, minced
1 cup extra-virgin olive oil
2 large carrots, shredded
4 large celery ribs, thinly sliced
3 tablespoons finely chopped fresh flat-leaf parsley

1. Clean the octopus by finding the beak in the center of its body and cutting it off with a sharp knife. Put the octopus in a large pot and add enough salted water to cover by 1 inch. Add a wine cork, cover, and bring to a boil over high heat. Reduce the heat to medium-low and uncover. Cook at a steady simmer until the octopus is tender when pierced with the tip of a sharp knife and the suction cups are easily removed, 1½ to 2½ hours. Remove from the heat and let stand in the cooking liquid until completely cooled, about 3 hours. Drain and rinse under cold running water, rubbing off the skin and suction cups. Cut into bite-size pieces.

2. Meanwhile, put the scungilli in a large saucepan and add enough salted water to cover by 1 inch. Add a wine cork, cover, and bring to a boil over high heat. Reduce the heat to medium-low and cover. Cook at a steady simmer until the scungilli is tender when pierced with the tip of a sharp knife, 1½ to 2½ hours. Drain and rinse under cold running water. Let cool. Cut each piece of scungilli on a slight diagonal into thin slices, then into ¼-inch-wide strips.

3. Bring a large saucepan of salted water to a boil over high heat. Add the shrimp and cook just until they turn opaque and firm, 2 to 3 minutes. Drain and rinse under cold running water.

4. Whisk the lemon juice and garlic together in a large bowl. Gradually whisk in the oil. Add the octopus, scungilli, shrimp, carrots, celery, and parsley. Mix well and season with salt. Cover and refrigerate until chilled, at least 4 hours or up to 3 days. Stir well and reseason with salt and lemon juice before serving chilled.

✱ ✱ ✱ Scungilli ✱ ✱ ✱

Scungilli, also called whelk, is a sea snail in a beautiful shell. It's a very Italian ingredient, closely related to the conch that's popular in the Caribbean and West Indies, where they eat it deep-fried, steamed, and curried. If you've never tried it, now's the time. Like octopus, it's usually only found fresh or frozen at specialty or Italian grocery stores, although you can get it canned—just don't tell my mother!

You can buy it cleaned or with its black "foot"—the part that acts as a door to shut its shell—still attached. My recommendation: go for fresh, already cleaned. Almost any way though, and it's delicious!

Another reason to give it a try? Scungilli is supposedly an amazing aphrodisiac. You've been warned.

✱ ✱ ✱ The Great Wine Cork Debate ✱ ✱ ✱

Italians, especially Italian mothers and grandmothers, always add a wine cork to the water to tenderize octopus. It's supposed to have something to do with the enzymes in the cork. It's never been scientifically proven or disproven, but my mother swears by it and so does Mario Batali. If anything, it gives you an excuse to open a bottle of wine. Cheers to that!

Summer Salad with Roasted Garlic Vinaigrette

Makes 6 to 8 servings

It's no secret that I love garlic, but I love-love-love *roasted* garlic. It just somehow tastes different; the roasting gives the garlic a mellow, almost nutty flavor. And it makes a *great* salad dressing. This is another one of my favorite summer salads. The combination of the sweet berries and spicy basil mixed with the mellow dressing is fabulicious!

Roasted Garlic:

1 full head of garlic, husk removed and separated into individual cloves
1 tablespoon extra-virgin olive oil
Pinch of salt

Dressing:

2 tablespoons balsamic vinegar
1 tablespoon fresh lemon juice
½ cup extra-virgin olive oil
Salt and freshly ground black pepper

Salad:

1 (5-ounce) bag of mixed baby greens
2 cups sliced strawberries
1 cup halved cherry tomatoes
1 cup packed whole basil leaves
⅓ cup pine nuts, toasted (see page 192)

1. To roast the garlic in the oven: Preheat the oven to 400°F. Place the garlic cloves in a large custard cup or small baking dish, drizzle with oil, and sprinkle with salt. Cover tightly with aluminum foil. Bake until the garlic is dark beige and very tender, about 45 minutes. Uncover and let the garlic cool completely.

To roast the garlic on a grill: Preheat the grill for indirect cooking with medium-high heat (400°F). Place the garlic cloves on a 12-inch square of aluminum foil, drizzle with oil, and sprinkle with salt. Fold the foil to enclose the garlic into a packet. Place on the turned-off area of the grill and close the lid. Cook until the garlic is very tender, about 45 minutes. Open the foil and let the garlic cool completely.

2. To make the dressing: Squeeze the flesh from each cooled clove into a blender. Add the vinegar and lemon juice and process until the garlic is pureed. With the machine running, gradually add the oil through the hole in the lid. Season with salt and pepper. (The dressing can be covered and refrigerated for up to 1 day.)

3. To make the salad: Toss the baby greens, strawberries, tomatoes, basil, and pine nuts with the dressing. Serve immediately.

Tomato and Baby Bocconcini Salad with Pesto Dressing

Makes 4 to 6 servings

This salad has all of the flavors of a Caprese salad, but this version is even more fun to eat because of the miniature tomatoes and bite-sized mozzarella balls. When you can find them, multicolored cherry tomatoes really make this salad look spectacular. The mixture is delicious with just about any kind of salad greens, but the peppery flavor of arugula makes it an Italian classic.

2 tablespoons Homemade Pesto
　　(page 161)
1 tablespoon red wine vinegar
¼ cup extra-virgin olive oil
1 pint cherry tomatoes,
　　cut into halves
8 ounces baby bocconchini or
　　ciliegine mozzarella balls
4 cups (about 3 ounces) baby
　　arugula or mixed salad greens
Salt and freshly ground
　　black pepper

1. Whisk the pesto, vinegar, and oil together in a large bowl to combine. Add the cherry tomatoes and mozzarella balls and season with salt and pepper. Mix well and let stand at room temperature until the tomatoes give off some juice, about 1½ hours.

2. Add the arugula, toss well, and season again with salt and pepper. Serve immediately.

✳ ✳ ✳ Little Mouthfuls ✳ ✳ ✳

Sometimes instead of slicing or grating mozzarella from a larger piece, you'd like smaller, bite-sized balls for your dish. For this reason, cheese makers created *bocconcini*—which means "little mouthfuls" in Italian—egg-size balls of mozzarella. Even smaller balls, the size of grapes, are called *bambini* (or "baby") bocconcini. There are also "cherry-size" balls called *ciliegine di mozzarella*. If you can't find any of these miniature sizes, you can always cut large fresh mozzarella balls into ½-inch cubes.

Italian Gazpacho

Makes 6 servings

You can't go through summer without having at least one bowl of chilled gazpacho made with juicy local tomatoes. This is my version, which has balsamic vinegar and fresh basil (or oregano) to give it an Italian feeling. Some people like it smooth, and some like it chunky. It really doesn't matter, as long as you use great tomatoes. Instead of croutons, serve it with wide slices of grilled bread alongside.

2 pounds plum (Roma) tomatoes, cored and seeded

1 large red bell pepper, cored, seeded, and very coarsely chopped

3/4 cup coarsely chopped red onion (about 1/2 medium onion)

1/3 cup packed fresh basil, plus chopped fresh basil for serving

3 garlic cloves, crushed under the flat side of a large knife and peeled

1/2 cup extra-virgin olive oil, plus more for serving

3 tablespoons balsamic vinegar

1/4 teaspoon red pepper flakes

Salt

1. Combine the tomatoes, bell pepper, red onion, basil, and garlic in a food processor. Pulse until the mixture is coarsely chopped. Add the oil, vinegar, and red pepper flakes, and pulse until the gazpacho is your desired texture. Season with salt. Transfer to a large bowl, cover, and refrigerate until chilled, at least 4 hours or overnight.

2. Ladle the gazpacho into soup bowls. Sprinkle each with basil and drizzle with oil. Serve cold.

* * * Tomatoes and Skin Care * * *

We know that tomatoes are good for our bodies, since they contain lycopene, but did you know they're also great for your skin? The same natural pigment that helps protect the tomato's skin from the harsh rays of the sun can also protect yours. While you should still wear full SPF sunscreen, lycopene can help protect your skin from within. Crushed tomato can also be applied to your face to soothe sunburn, clear up acne, and dry out oily patches.

Summary Minestrone

Makes 10 to 12 servings

Americans might think of minestrone as a cold-weather soup, but in Italy, it's made year-round. In the summer, I use local vegetables to make an incredible vegetarian soup that you can even serve chilled—just as they do in Italy when the weather is hot. This purposely makes a huge batch because the soup only gets better with age, and it is a beautiful thing to have a big container of soup in the fridge for a quick meal.

2 tablespoons extra-virgin olive oil, plus more for serving

1 medium onion, chopped

3 medium carrots, cut into ½-inch dice

3 medium celery ribs, cut into ½-inch dice

2 garlic cloves, minced

4 ripe plum (Roma) tomatoes, cored, seeded, and diced

2 tablespoons chopped fresh flat-leaf parsley

1 tablespoon chopped fresh oregano

2 medium zucchini, cut into ½-inch dice

1 medium yellow squash, cut into ½-inch dice

1 (15.5-ounce) can white kidney (cannellini) beans, drained and rinsed

1 (15.5-ounce) can pink or Roman beans, drained and rinsed

Salt and freshly ground black pepper

Homemade Pesto (page 161), for serving

1. Heat the oil in a soup pot over medium heat. Add the onion, carrots, and celery and cook, stirring occasionally, until they begin to soften, about 5 minutes. Stir in the garlic and cook until fragrant, about 1 minute. Stir in 7 cups of water, the tomatoes, parsley, and oregano and bring to a boil. Reduce the heat to medium-low and simmer until the vegetables are tender, about 45 minutes.

2. Add the zucchini, yellow squash, white beans, and pink beans and bring to a simmer over high heat. Return the heat to medium-low and simmer until the zucchini is tender, about 10 minutes. Season with salt and pepper. (The soup can be cooled, covered, and refrigerated for up to 2 days.)

3. Ladle into soup bowls and top each serving with about a teaspoon of pesto and a drizzle of olive oil. Serve hot, warm, chilled, or at room temperature.

CHAPTER 5

Carne (Meat)

Tutto fumo e niente arrosto.

Instead of saying that something is no big deal or
someone is "all bark and no bite," Italians say
it's "all smoke and no roast."

O f all the things that people grill, meat is the most common—and the most commonly messed up! We're going to fix that once and for all, so your burgers will be perfect, your steak will cut like butter, and your pork chops will be to-die-for delicious.

The most important thing to remember is that you're not always going to cook everything over high heat. As my Joe says, "Take it nice and slow." It's called "grilling," not "burning."

THE TRUTH ABOUT TENDERIZING

One of the biggest mistakes people make is trying to tenderize their meat in all the wrong ways. When I see someone pull out a metal hammer that looks like a medieval torture device and start hacking away at the raw steak, I cry a little inside. Believe it or not, tenderizing has nothing to do with hitting anything.

There are four main ways to truly tenderize meat: A) cooking it with moist, low heat for a long time to break down the tough parts; B) letting the meat tenderize naturally as its enzymes change, like butchers do by dry aging beef, but that takes about twenty days to work; C) using an actual tenderizing tool that looks like a metal spike to poke into meat to break up the gristle, but doing this also breaks the muscle and creates holes to let moisture escape; and D) choosing a good, tender cut to begin with. The best choice is D.

(And remember, the most tender doesn't always mean the most flavorful. Have you ever noticed the flavor difference between flank steak and filet mignon? Just because it's beef doesn't mean that every cut tastes the same.)

HAMMER TIME

If you use a pointy hammer on your steak in an attempt to tenderize it, you'll break up not only some of the connective tissue, but also the actual meat. Think of a meat hammer as a giant beast that is pre-chewing your steak for you. No good.

So what do people use a hammer for? To make a piece of meat—usually boneless and skinless chicken breast halves—a uniform thickness so it will cook evenly. If you have a giant hump on one end, that part won't get cooked through while the thinner end is overcooked. Steaks are usually pretty uniformly cut already, so you don't need to pound them; chicken usually isn't, so you do. But when you do, you should use a flat mallet or a rolling pin so you aren't damaging the meat. Put the meat between plastic storage bags, as this creates a slicker surface that helps the meat "stretch" from the pounding. And it's best to pound the meat when it's cold just after taking it out of the fridge, when the meat is firmer.

THE MARINADE MYTH

It's a myth that marinades can tenderize steak. They add great flavor and are good for your health when you're grilling (I'll tell you why in a minute), but they can't really penetrate a steak or the individual muscle fibers. It takes beef's natural enzymes almost a month to work on making steak soft during the dry-aging

✳ ✳ ✳ **Steak Selection Cheat Sheet** ✳ ✳ ✳

You don't have to buy a porterhouse to get tender steak. As long as you prep, cook, and cut it correctly, there are many inexpensive cuts that are juicy and delicious. But there are some, like round steak, that are best avoided on the grill unless you're a master and want to exercise your jaw muscles. There are a million choices, but here are my personal recommendations:

Expensive Cuts You Can't Go Wrong With:

—Tenderloin	—T-bone	—Porterhouse
—Top Loin	—Strip Steak	—Club Steak

Inexpensive Cuts That Are Great with Marinades:

—Sirloin	—Flank	—Chuck
—Round	—Tri-Tip	—Skirt

Inexpensive Cuts That Are Great with Careful Cutting Across the Grain:

—Flank	—Tri-Tip	—Flat Iron
—Skirt		

process; a few hours in your fridge isn't going to cut it. In fact, even if you marinate a steak for five days, it will only soak into the meat about one-eighth of an inch.

PRECOOKING TEMPERATURE

You might have heard that you need to bring meat to room temperature before cooking it, but that's a little too warm and not safe. All you need to do is take the chill off the refrigeration, which can be done in thirty minutes (on a hot day, you may only need fifteen). If you don't, and try and grill the cold meat right away, you'll end up having to increase your cooking time, which will decrease the deliciousness.

Covering your steak with plastic wrap while it sits on the counter doesn't do anything to help or hinder it, either. You really don't need to unless you have a dog that might run in and snatch it, or if there are pesky flies around.

FORKED

Did you notice what *isn't* on my list of the tools you needed for grilling (see page 25). A grilling fork. Not only do you *not need* one, but you also *shouldn't* use one. Ever. Turn your meat with long tongs. If you pierce it with anything to pick it up, you're putting holes in it. It's the equivalent of stabbing your steak in its prime and watching its life essence drip away. . .

Now, I didn't say to use a spatula to flip your meat, and here's why: it's far too tempting to use the back of the spatula to press down on the meat before you flip it, especially burgers. Doing so may make that cool sizzling sound from fat dripping onto the flames, but it's a serious grilling offense. Not only does it rob the meat of moisture, leaving it more likely to dry out, but it can also cause a dangerous flare-up. So why do we do it so much if we're not supposed to? A friend told me it's because we've seen it done on TV and in restaurants: the cooks squish the burgers. But those are flat, mass-produced burgers that need to get off the grill in a hurry, and are almost always served medium-well to well done.

PREMATURE FLIPPING AND TOO MUCH FUSSING

Another thing that can ruin your otherwise perfect piece of meat or patty: moving it around too much. You only want to flip it once. Don't go near the meat until the underside has formed a nice crust. This is true of all grilling, but it's especially true with burgers because too much flipping can make the patty fall apart.

COOKING TEMPS

When you remove food from the grill, it keeps cooking inside so the internal temperature will actually go up three to five degrees. For that reason, you should take your meat off the grill when it measures three to five degrees before your desired temperature so it will end up right where you want it. So if you want a medium steak, take it off the grill at 130°F, let it rest, and it will go up to 135°F.

Here's a handy chart of what temperatures correspond to our descriptions of rare through well done meat.

* * * **Optimum Temperature After Resting:** * * *

Rare = 120°F to 130°F

Medium-Rare = 130°F to 135°F

Medium = 135°F to 140°F

Medium-Well = 140°F to 145°F

Well = Over 145°F

THE IMPORTANCE OF REST

Another thing that people tend to rush is serving the meat after it's cooked. You must, must, must let it rest first. After you take it off the grill, let it stand undisturbed for at least 5 minutes, 10 minutes for larger pieces. It won't get cold (in fact it will keep cooking), but it will get much, much juicier. When meat is heated, all the moisture is forced out of the meat fibers and settles in the middle. Cut it open right away, and the precious juices will flood your plate. When you let it rest, you give the meat fibers a chance to relax, open back up, and reabsorb the moisture throughout, making every single bite—as long as you're patient!—a luscious, lip-smacking wonder.

THE TOUCH TEST

Not all cuts of meats—thin pork chops and steaks and chicken breast—are thick enough for you to use a thermometer. (That's one reason why a thin-stemmed, instant-read thermometer is better than a thick-stemmed, old-fashioned thermometer.) If you don't have a thermometer, you could always slice into the meat to see how done it is, but that's really ugly and lets the juices out, and really, just don't do that. Instead, get to know your way around steak by learning how to tell how done it is inside by the "touch test." If you poke the steak in the middle with your forefinger, you can tell its degree of doneness by how firm or soft it is. How do you gauge what's firm and what's soft? It's takes some practice, but here's how it works:

Open your left hand so that your palm is facing up. Keep it nice and relaxed, then poke the fleshy part under your thumb with the forefinger (the first finger, also called your "index" or "pointer" finger, depending on where you grew up) on your right hand. See how squishy that is? That's how "raw" feels.

Now touch your left thumb to your left forefinger, making a loose "o" shape.

Poke the fleshy part of your thumb with your right forefinger again. This time it's a little firmer. That's what "rare" feels like.

Now release that finger, and touch your left thumb to your left middle finger. Poke yourself. A little firmer. That's "medium-rare."

I think you know where we're going with this: Touching your left thumb to your left ring finger and poking your fleshy bit is what "medium" cooked meat feels like.

And finally, your left thumb touching your left pinkie gives you the same tension as "well-done" meat.

Chi la vuole cotta e chi la vuole cruda.

Literally: "Some want it cooked,
and some want it raw."
What it means: "Different strokes for different folks."

Steak Milanese

Makes 4 servings

This simple dish is as Italian as they come. We just call it "beef cutlets"; it's breaded steak on the grill. In fact, it's the first recipe Joe told me I had to include in this book because we make it so much. The breading helps keep the steak juicy and delicious! This is one time when you don't want to cook the steak over high, but over medium heat to crisp the crust. For "chicken cutlets," just substitute the steak with pounded boneless and skinless chicken breast halves, and cook for about 10 minutes total.

1½ pounds sirloin steak, trimmed,
    cut 1 inch thick
2 tablespoons extra-virgin olive oil
¾ teaspoon salt
½ teaspoon freshly ground
    black pepper
½ cup Italian-seasoned
    dry bread crumbs
Freshly grated Parmesan cheese,
    for serving
Lemon wedges, for serving

1. Cut the steak into 4 serving portions. Using the flat side of a meat mallet, pound the meat until it is about ½ inch thick, or about half of its original thickness.

2. Brush the steaks generously on both sides with the oil and season with the salt and pepper. Spread the bread crumbs on a plate. Coat the steaks with the bread crumbs, patting them into the steaks to help them adhere. Let stand at room temperature while preheating the grill.

3. Preheat the grill for direct cooking over medium heat (400°F).

4. Holding with long tongs, use a wad of paper towels dipped in olive oil to grease the cooking grate. Place the steaks on the cooking grate and close the grill lid. Cook the steaks until the breading on the underside is crisp and browned, about 2½ minutes. Flip the steaks and continue cooking, with the lid closed, until the other sides are browned, about 2½ minutes more for medium-rare steaks. Remove from the grill. Sprinkle with the Parmesan. Let stand 5 minutes. Serve hot, with the lemon wedges.

✳ ✳ ✳ Homemade Bread Crumbs ✳ ✳ ✳

If you've read my other *Fabulicious* cookbooks, you know that Italians do not like to waste food. We cook with and eat as much of the plant and animal as we can (herb-seasoned sausage is the perfect example). We like to keep the bones in our cooking for extra flavor. And we have tons of uses for stale bread: bruschetta, crostini, soups, panzanella salads, and of course, bread crumbs.

Canned bread crumbs are great (and will keep in the freezer for up to a year!), but if you want to make your own using stale (or not-so-stale) bread slices, here's how: Cut the crusts off, pull the slices into 1-inch pieces, and place in a food processor. Pulse for a couple minutes until you have coarse crumbs. Don't overprocess them though; the goal is crumbs, not flour. Three slices of sandwich-sized bread will make about 1 cup of bread crumbs.

To make your bread crumbs "Italian-style," simply add your favorite Italian herbs to the mix. For every cup of bread crumbs, add 1 fresh basil leaf (or ¼ teaspoon dried basil), 1 sprig fresh parsley (or ½ teaspoon dried parsley), ½ teaspoon salt, ½ teaspoon ground black pepper, and ½ teaspoon garlic powder.

Store the breadcrumbs in an airtight container in the freezer for up to 3 months.

Grilled Steak Pizzaiola

Makes 4 servings

This is kind of like the Steak Pizzaiola that I make indoors, but the sizzle of the grill adds even more flavor to one of my favorite dishes. In this version, I use fresh summer tomatoes to make a sauce instead of canned, and fresh herbs instead of dried—not that I would ever use dried parsley anyway since it tastes like dead leaves from your doorstep. This sauce is just enough for the steak, but you can easily double it to go over a pound of pasta. Roasted red peppers set it off.

Summer Tomato Sauce:

2 tablespoons extra-virgin olive oil

1 small onion, finely chopped

2 garlic cloves, minced

1 pound plum (Roma) tomatoes, cored, seeded, and diced

1/4 teaspoon red pepper flakes

Salt

1 tablespoon chopped fresh oregano or basil or 1 teaspoon dried oregano

1 tablespoon chopped fresh flat-leaf parsley

1. To make the sauce: Heat the oil in a medium saucepan over medium heat. Add the onion and cook, stirring occasionally until softened, about 3 minutes. Stir in garlic and cook until fragrant, about 1 minute. Add the tomatoes, 1/4 cup water, and red pepper flakes. Season with salt. Cook until the tomatoes give off their juices, about 5 minutes. Reduce the heat to medium-low and simmer, stirring occasionally, about 20 minutes, until the sauce thickens. During the last 5 minutes, stir in the oregano and parsley. Remove from the heat and cover to keep warm.

> ✳ ✳ ✳ **Greasing the Grate** ✳ ✳ ✳
>
> Besides grilling pizza, this is the one time where I will let you oil the grill to help keep the breaded food from sticking. To do this, dip a wad of paper towels in olive oil, pinch it in long-handled tongs, and lightly brush it over the grate. Don't overdo it, though; you just want enough to grease the grate, not so much that it is dripping into the flames, which could cause dangerous flare-ups.

Steak:

2 shell (strip) steaks (12 ounces
  each and cut ¾ inch thick)

Extra-virgin olive oil

¾ teaspoon salt

½ teaspoon freshly
  ground black pepper

2 large red bell peppers, roasted
  and skinned (see Grilling
  Peppers, page 178),
  cut into ½-inch-thick strips

Chopped fresh parsley, for garnish

2. To make the steaks: Meanwhile, brush the steaks on both sides with oil and season with the salt and pepper. Let stand at room temperature while preheating the grill.

3. Preheat the grill for direct cooking over high heat (500°F).

4. Place the steaks on the cooking grate and close the grill lid. Cook until the underside is browned and seared with grill marks, about 3 minutes. Flip the steaks and cook, with the lid closed, until the other side is browned and the steak feels somewhat soft with little resistance when pressed on top with a fingertip, 3 to 4 minutes more for medium-rare. Remove from the grill. Transfer the steaks to a carving board and let stand 5 minutes.

5. Cut the steak across the grain into diagonal ½-inch-thick slices. Spread the tomato sauce on a deep platter. Add the sliced steak and the carving juices. Top with the roasted red pepper strips. Sprinkle with the parsley and serve hot.

Teresa's Tip

To avoid a prep crunch, grill, cool, and peel the peppers an hour or so before grilling the steak.

Flank Steak alla Sala Consilina

Makes 4 to 6 servings

The secret to this recipe—tomato paste—makes the marinade nice and thick, and helps create a beautiful crust on the steak during grilling. Flank steak is a very lean cut that will get tough if you cook it more than medium-rare, though, so if you like well-done meat, make something else! Try this marinade with other steaks, such as skirt or sirloin.

Red Wine Marinade:

1 cup hearty red wine,
    such as Shiraz
1/3 cup extra-virgin olive oil
1/4 cup balsamic vinegar
1/4 cup tomato paste
2 tablespoons finely chopped
    fresh basil
2 teaspoons dried oregano
3 garlic cloves, finely chopped
1/2 teaspoon salt
1/2 teaspoon freshly
    ground black pepper

Steak:

1 flank steak (about 1 3/4 pounds and
    1 inch thick)

1. To make the marinade: Whisk all of the ingredients together in a medium bowl until tomate paste is dissolved.

2. Put the steak in a 1-gallon resealable plastic bag. Pour in the marinade and close the bag. Refrigerate, occasionally turning the bag, for at least 4 and up to 12 hours. Let stand at room temperature for 30 minutes before grilling.

3. Preheat the grill for direct cooking over very high heat (500°F).

4. To make the steak: Remove the steak from the marinade, shaking off the excess, and discard the marinade. Place the steak on the cooking grate and close the grill lid. Cook the steak until the underside is browned and seared with grill marks, about 4 minutes. Flip the steak and continue cooking, with the lid closed, until the other side is browned and the steak feel somewhat soft with little resistance when pressed on top with a fingertip, about 4 minutes more for medium-rare. Transfer the steak to a carving board and let stand for 5 minutes.

5. Cut the steak across the grain at a slight diagonal into thin slices. Transfer to a platter, pour the juices on top, and serve hot.

* * * Cutting Against the Grain * * *

You can cook flank steak perfectly, but if you slice it incorrectly after it comes off the grill, you'll ruin all that tenderness. How can you avoid this? Cut against the grain, not with it.

Cutting along the same lines as the muscle fibers (or "the grain" of the meat) will just separate the individual fibers, but leave a lot of them intact, and tough. If you cut against the grain (at a forty-five-degree angle to the lines or at least diagonal to them), you're slicing up the tough muscle, not the soft connectors between them, and you'll have a melt-in-your-mouth result.

Try to cut it as thinly as possible, about ¼ inch thick or thinner. Be sure your knife is thin and good and sharp; a serrated or dull knife will just tear up your meat. And make sure you're looking at the actual grain of the meat and not the marks from your grill! (It sounds silly, but I've seen it done!)

Mare e Monti (Surf and Turf)

Makes 4 servings

Use any steak you like for this. I use club steak (which is a 1 pound shell steak cut in half to make two smaller steaks about 8 ounces each), but for a special occasion, you could use filet mignon. The idea here is to grill the steaks and shrimp, pile some shrimp on each steak, and top the stack with a big spoon of garlic butter. Be sure that the garlic butter is at room temperature and really soft so it will melt over the food without cooling it down.

Garlic Butter:

6 tablespoons (¾ stick) unsalted butter, at room temperature

2 garlic cloves, crushed through a garlic press

1 tablespoon fresh lemon juice

1 tablespoon finely chopped fresh flat-leaf parsley

1 tablespoon finely chopped fresh chives or scallion greens

Steak and Shrimp:

4 club steaks (each 8 ounces and cut 1 inch thick)

1¼ teaspoons salt, divided

1¼ teaspoons freshly ground black pepper, divided

2 tablespoons finely chopped fresh rosemary

24 large (21 to 25 count) shrimp, about 1¼ pounds, peeled and deveined with tail segment left attached

1 tablespoon extra-virgin olive oil

1. To make the garlic butter: Using a rubber spatula, mash and mix all of the ingredients together in a small bowl until combined. Set aside at room temperature for at least 1 and up to 4 hours.

2. To make the steak: Season the steaks on both sides with 1 teaspoon of salt and 1 teaspoon of pepper, then rub with the rosemary. Let stand at room temperature for 30 minutes.

3. To make the shrimp: Toss the shrimp and olive oil with the remaining ¼ teaspoon salt and ¼ teaspoon in pepper in a large bowl.

4. Preheat the grill for direct cooking over high heat (500°F).

5. Place the steaks on one side of the grill. Put a perforated grill pan next to the steaks. Close the lid and cook until the undersides of the steaks are browned and seared with grill marks, about 4 minutes. Flip the steaks and continue cooking, with the lid closed, until an instant-read thermometer inserted horizontally through

> ### Teresa's Tip
> Shrimp are much easier to grill on a perforated grill pan than directly on the grate.

the side into the center of a steak reads 125°F, 3 to 4 minutes more for medium-rare. Transfer the steaks to a platter and tent with aluminum foil.

6. Add the shrimp to the perforated grill pan and spread in a single layer. Close the grill lid. Cook until the shrimp are turning opaque around the edges, 2 to 3 minutes. Flip the shrimp and continue cooking, with the lid closed, until they are completely opaque, about 2 minutes more. Transfer the shrimp to a plate.

7. For each serving, place a steak on a dinner plate and top with 6 shrimp. Add a dollop of the garlic butter over each mound of shrimp. Serve hot.

✳ ✳ ✳ From the Sea to the Mountains ✳ ✳ ✳

A meal that includes both steak and seafood is called "surf and turf" in English, but not in most other languages. Why? Because when translated, it not as catchy. "Surf" in Italian is *cresta dell'onda*, and turf is *zolla erbosa*. Ordering *cresta dell'onda e zolla erbosa* wouldn't be much fun, nor would it fit on anyone's menu. Instead, in Italy, to get a steak and seafood combination, you'd ask for *mare e monti,* which basically means the same thing, but doesn't sound as pretty in English: "sea and mountains."

Marinated Short Ribs with Red Wine Sauce

Makes 6 servings

This might seem like a lot of steps, but they're super easy, can be done way ahead of the final grilling, and you will love every bite. Like really, really love. Buy individual meaty short ribs (the kind that are on a single bone and sometimes called "English cut") and not the crosscut, Korean-style, or flanken ribs.

Red Wine and Herb Marinade:

1½ cups hearty red wine,
   such as Shiraz
½ cup extra-virgin olive oil
1 small onion, cut into
   thin half-moons
⅓ cup red wine vinegar
2 tablespoons tomato paste
2 teaspoons finely chopped
   fresh thyme
3 garlic cloves, minced
3 bay leaves
1 teaspoon salt
½ teaspoon red pepper flakes

Short Ribs:

12 meaty short ribs,
   about 5½ pounds
Extra-virgin olive oil
2 tablespoons tomato paste
2 tablespoons light brown sugar
Salt and freshly ground
   black pepper

1. **To make the marinade:** Whisk all of the ingredients together in a medium bowl until tomato paste is dissolved.

2. **To make the ribs:** Divide the short ribs and marinade between two 1-gallon resealable plastic bags, and close the bags. Refrigerate, occasionally turning the bags, for at least 2 and up to 4 hours.

3. Preheat the grill for indirect cooking over medium (400°F) heat.

4. Lightly oil a large disposable aluminum foil roasting pan large enough to hold the short ribs in a single layer. Arrange the short ribs in the pan and pour in the marinade. Place the pan with the short ribs directly over the ignited burner(s) and bring the cooking liquid to a simmer. Cover the pan tightly with aluminum foil. Move to the unlit burner(s) and close the lid. Cook for 1 hour. Uncover the pan and turn the ribs over. Cover again with the foil and continue cooking until the ribs are tender when pierced with the tip of a knife, about 1 hour more. (You can also bake the ribs in a preheated 350°F oven, turning them after 1 hour, until tender, about 2 hours total.)

5. Transfer the short ribs to a platter and set aside. Strain the cooking liquid into a medium saucepan. Bring to a boil over high heat over high heat (or use the side burner on your grill, if you have one). Cook, stirring often, until reduced by half, about 10 minutes. Whisk in the tomato paste and brown sugar and cook until lightly thickened, about 2 minutes more. The short ribs and sauce can be stored at room temperature for up to 1½ hours, or cooled, covered, and refrigerated for up to 8 hours.

6. Preheat the grill for direct cooking over medium heat (400°F).

7. Lightly brush the short ribs with olive oil. Season with salt and pepper. Place the ribs directly on the cooking grate and close the grill lid. Cook, turning occasionally, with the lid closed as much as possible, until the meat is lightly crusted and browned, about 5 minutes. Brush with some of the sauce and continue cooking and turning until glazed, about 3 minutes more. Return to the platter. Drizzle with the remaining sauce and serve hot.

Giudice Burgers with Peppers and Gorgonzola

Makes 4 servings

Joe loves to mix things into raw ground beef and then form patties to make burgers that taste great with every bite. The vegetables in the ground beef will heat up more quickly than the raw meat, so it is difficult to get this to cook less than medium. They are so flavorful that you won't really need any additional condiments. To keep the burger juicy, we use ground round, which has more fat than sirloin.

1 tablespoon extra-virgin olive oil,
    plus more for brushing

1 medium onion, finely chopped

1 small red bell pepper, cored and
    cut into 1/4-inch dice

1 garlic clove, minced

1 1/2 pounds ground round beef

1 teaspoon salt

1/2 teaspoon freshly ground
    black pepper

4 ounces Gorgonzola cheese, cut
    into eight 1/4-inch thick slices

4 hamburger buns

4 tomato slices

4 red lettuce leaves

✳ ✳ ✳ Rare Giudice Burgers ✳ ✳ ✳

If you like rare burgers, skip the onion mixture, grill the burgers for 6 minutes, top with cheese during the last minute, and serve with grilled red peppers (see page 180).

1. Heat the oil in a medium skillet over medium heat. Add the onion and red pepper and cook, stirring occasionally, until very tender, about 10 minutes. During the last minute of cooking, stir in the garlic. Remove from the heat and let cool completely.

2. Gently but thoroughly mix the ground round, cooled vegetable mixture, salt, and pepper well with your hands in a large bowl. Shape the meat mixture into four 4-inch patties. (Don't compact the meat or the burgers will be tough.). Let stand at room temperature while preheating the grill.

3. Preheat the grill for direct cooking over medium-high heat (450°F).

4. Lightly brush both sides of the patties with oil. Place the patties on the cooking grate and close the grill lid. Cook until the undersides are browned, about 3 minutes. Flip the burgers and continue cooking, with the lid closed, until the other sides are browned and the burger feels slightly resistent when pressed on top with a fingertip, about 3 minutes more for medium. During the last minute, top each burger with two Gorgonzola slices. Remove from the grill.

5. Place the buns on the grill and cook, with the lid closed, turning once, until lightly toasted, about 1 minute.

6. For each serving, place a burger on bun bottom. Top with a tomato slice, a lettuce leaf, and the burger top, and serve.

Pork and Vegetable Spiedini

Makes 4 servings

These Italian skewers are super easy and—with a marinade of lemon, garlic, herbs, and olive oil—super delicious. Just don't shove the pieces onto the sticks too closely together so that the heat can circulate and cook everything. When checking for doneness, the pork should look a little rare when pierced with a knife. It will continue cooking off the grill.

Special equipment:
4 metal grilling skewers

Lemon-Herb Marinade:
½ cup extra-virgin olive oil
Finely grated zest of 1 lemon
¼ cup fresh lemon juice
2 teaspoons finely chopped
    fresh rosemary
2 teaspoons finely chopped
    fresh thyme
4 garlic cloves, crushed under the
    flat side of a knife and peeled
½ teaspoon salt
½ teaspoon red pepper flakes

Spiedini:
1½ pounds pork tenderloin,
    trimmed of fat and silver skin, cut
    into 16 pieces
1 medium red bell pepper, cored
    and cut into 16 pieces
1 medium yellow bell pepper, cored
    and cut into 16 pieces
1 small zucchini, cut into 4 rounds
Extra virgin olive oil
1 teaspoon salt
½ teaspoon freshly ground
    black pepper

1. To make the marinade: Whisk the ingredients together in a medium bowl.

2. To make the spiedini: Place the pork in a 1-gallon resealable plastic bag. Pour in the marinade and close the bag. Refrigerate, turning occasionally, for 30 minutes to 1 hour, no longer.

3. Remove the pork from the marinade, shaking off the excess, and discard the marinade. For each serving, thread 4 pieces of pork, 2 each of red and yellow peppers, and 1 piece of zucchini, alternating them on the skewer as desired. Do not crowd the ingredients on the skewer. Brush the pork and vegetables with olive oil and season with the salt and pepper. Let stand while preheating the grill.

4. Preheat the grill for direct cooking over medium heat (400°F).

5. Place the kebabs directly on the cooking grate and close the lid. Cook, turning about every 3 minutes, with the lid closed as much as possible, until the pork is browned and shows a hint of pink when pierced to the skewer with the tip of a knife, 12 to 15 minutes. Remove the kebabs from the grill. Let stand 5 minutes. Remove the skewers and serve hot.

Pancetta-Wrapped Pork Loin

Makes 6 to 8 servings

Bacon without the smoke, pancetta is Italian soul food. Its fat moistens lean food like pork loin, and when grilled it will create a crusty coating. Look for pancetta at your local Italian deli or specialty supermarket. Ask for it to be cut about ⅛-inch thick. You will need to tie the pancetta onto the pork roast with kitchen twine (or you can even use unwaxed, unflavored dental floss!).

1 center-cut boneless pork loin roast (about 2¾ pounds), excess fat trimmed

1 teaspoon salt

½ teaspoon freshly ground black pepper

2 tablespoons extra-virgin olive oil

4 garlic cloves, minced

2 teaspoons finely chopped fresh thyme

2 teaspoons finely chopped fresh sage

2 teaspoons red wine vinegar

8 ounces (⅛-inch-thick) sliced pancetta, about 16 slices

1. Cut the pork horizontally through the center, reaching almost, but not quite to the other side. Open up the pork like a book. Season all over with the salt and pepper.

2. Mix the oil, garlic, thyme, sage, and vinegar together in a small bowl. Spread the herb paste on the cut surface of the pork. Close the pork. Unroll each strip of pancetta. Arrange half of the pancetta over the top of the roast. Using kitchen twine, tie the pancetta crosswise in a few places, leaving the ends of the roast uncovered. Turn the roast over (don't worry if it doesn't look neat). Repeat with the remaining pancetta. Let stand at room temperature for 30 minutes. Place the roast on a roasting rack in a metal roasting pan.

3. Preheat the grill for indirect cooking with medium (400°F) heat.

4. Place the pork in the roasting pan over the unheated burner(s) and close the grill lid. Cook, turning the pork about every 15 minutes, until the pancetta is crisp and browned and an instant-read thermometer inserted in the center of the roast reads 145°F, about 1¼ hours. Transfer the pork to a cutting board and let stand 10 minutes.

5. Remove the strings. Cut crosswise into ½-inch-thick slices and transfer to a serving platter. Pour the carving juices on top and serve hot.

Apple-Stuffed Pork Chops

Makes 4 servings

Pork chops are a great, inexpensive cut of meat—unless you grill them plain and overcook them, which will make them tasteless and tough. Marinating them in apple cider, stuffing them with an apple and onion filling, and then grilling them will give you a guaranteed succulent summer feast. If you like blue cheese, you can add ¼ cup (about 1 ounce) crumbled Gorgonzola to the cooled apple stuffing.

Apple and Herb Marinade:

1½ cups apple cider or apple juice

⅓ cup cider vinegar

⅓ cup extra-virgin olive oil

2 garlic cloves, minced

2 teaspoons finely chopped
   fresh sage

2 teaspoons finely chopped
   fresh thyme

2 bay leaves

1 teaspoon salt

½ teaspoon freshly
   ground black pepper

Pork Chops:

4 bone-in double-cut pork chops
   (each about 12 ounces)

1 tablespoon extra-virgin olive oil

1 medium onion, chopped

1 Granny Smith apple, unpeeled,
   shredded down to the core on
   the large holes of a box grater

Salt and freshly ground
   black pepper

1. To make the marinade: Whisk all of the ingredients together in a medium bowl.

2. To make the pork chops: One at a time, using a small sharp knife and starting at the fatty side, cut a deep pocket horizontally into each chop. Put the pork chops into a 1-gallon resealable plastic bag. Pour in the marinade and close the bag. Refrigerate, occasionally turning the bag, for 1 to 2 hours.

3. Meanwhile, heat the 1 tablespoon of olive oil in a medium skillet over medium heat. Add the onion and cook, stirring occasionally, until golden, about 6 minutes. Add the shredded apple and cook until heated through, about 2 minutes. Season with salt and pepper. Remove from the heat and let cool.

4. Remove the chops from the marinade, shaking off the excess, and discard the marinade. Pat the chops dry with paper towels. Fill the pocket in each chop with the apple mixture. Let stand at room temperature while preheating the grill.

5. Preheat the grill for direct cooking over medium heat (400°F).

6. Place the chops on the cooking grate and close the grill lid. Cook the chops until the undersides are browned and seared with grill marks, about 7 minutes. Flip the chops and continue cooking, with the lid closed, until the chops show no sign of pink when pierced at the bone with the tip of a sharp knife, 7 to 10 minutes more. Remove the chops from the grill. Let stand 5 minutes. Serve hot.

---

* * * Orchard Pigs * * *

Why do pork and apples taste so good together? Maybe it's because of the old saying "what grows together, goes together." In Italy, pigs are kept for year-round meat because they are low maintenance: you let them forage around and go fetch them when you're hungry. Pigs would roam the woods and orchards, eating the apples that fell on the ground, so the taste pairing could actually be from the inside out, as well!

Italian Spareribs

Makes 6 servings

Spareribs don't have to be a sticky, sweet mess. My version is *molto Italiano* (very Italian), with fresh sage, garlic, bay leaves, fennel, and of course red pepper flakes. These are great served with my Patata Rossa (Red Potato) Salad and Summer Salad with Roasted Garlic Vinaigrette on pages 71 and 74.

Very Italian Marinade:

1½ cups dry white wine,
    such as Pinot Grigio

½ cup extra-virgin olive oil

⅓ cup fresh lemon juice

2 tablespoons finely chopped
    fresh sage

1 teaspoon ground fennel seed
    (crushed with a mortar and
    pestle or under a heavy skillet)

3 garlic cloves, minced

3 bay leaves

1 teaspoon salt

½ teaspoon red pepper flakes

Spareribs

5 pounds pork spareribs,
    cut into 4 slabs

1. To make the marinade: Whisk all of the ingredients together in a medium bowl.

2. To make the ribs: Evenly divide the spareribs and marinade between two 1-gallon resealable plastic bags and close the bags. Refrigerate, turning the bags occasionally, for at least 2 and up to 6 hours. Remove from the refrigerator and let stand for 30 minutes before grilling.

3. Preheat the grill for indirect cooking with medium-low heat (350°F).

4. Remove the spareribs from the marinade, shaking off the excess, and discard the marinade. Place the spareribs over the unignited burner(s) and close the grill lid. Cook, turning the ribs every 30 minutes, until browned and tender (the meat will have shrunk from the ends of the bones), about 1¾ hours. Transfer the ribs to a carving board. Let stand 10 minutes. Cut between the bones into individual ribs and transfer to a platter. Serve hot.

Grilled Veal Chops
with Marsala Mushrooms

Makes 6 servings

It's time you learned how to make those big, thick veal chops that you get in a restaurant at home. To save time, you can make the mushrooms in advance. To take this over the top, add a dollop of room-temperature mascarpone or Parmesan curls (shaved right from a block of Parm with a vegetable peeler) over each chop just before serving. This is a great dish to serve when you have company.

Marsala Mushroooms:

2 tablespoons unsalted butter

10 ounces cremini (baby bella) mushrooms, sliced

1 small onion, finely chopped

1 tablespoon all-purpose flour

1/2 cup dry Marsala

1 cup reduced-sodium beef broth

1 tablespoon finely chopped fresh flat-leaf parsley

Salt and freshly ground black pepper

Veal Chops:

6 veal rib chops, each 12 to 14 ounces and cut 1 1/2 inches thick

Extra-virgin olive oil

1 1/4 teaspoons salt

3/4 teaspoon freshly ground black pepper

Finely chopped fresh flat-leaf parsley, for garnish

1. To make the mushrooms: Melt the butter in a large skillet over medium heat. Add the mushrooms and cook, stirring occasionally, until they give off their juices and begin to brown, about 10 minutes. Stir in the onion and cook, stirring occasionally, until it softens, about 2 minutes.

2. Sprinkle the flour over the mushroom mixture and stir well. Stir in the Marsala, followed by the broth and parsley, and bring to a boil. Cook, stirring often, until the liquid has thickened and reduced by half, about 5 minutes. Season with salt and pepper. Remove from the heat. (The mushrooms can be prepared up to 2 hours ahead, kept at room temperature. Reheat over low heat before serving.)

3. To make the veal chops: Brush the veal chops on both sides with oil. Season with the salt and pepper. Let stand at room temperature while preparing the grill.

4. Preheat the grill for direct cooking over medium heat (400°F).

5. Place the veal on the cooking grate grill and close the grill lid. Cook until the undersides are browned and seared with grill marks, about 7 minutes. Flip the veal chops and continue cooking, with the lid closed, until the veal shows a hint of pink when pierced at the bone with the tip of a sharp knife, 7 to 10 minutes more. Remove the chops from the grill. Let stand 5 minutes.

6. For each serving, place a veal chop on a dinner plate and top with parsley and a spoonful of the mushrooms. Serve hot.

✳ ✳ ✳ Vino Marsala ✳ ✳ ✳

When my parents emigrated from Salerno to America, they moved to New Jersey to live near other Italians. Growing up, our neighbors were from Sicily. They were big Marsala wine fans, as they should be—the true Italian wine can only be produced in the Marsala region of Sicily.

Marsala is a fortified wine, meaning that the winemakers add extra alcohol to it. While regular wine is around eleven percent alcohol, Marsala is closer to twenty percent. The extra alcohol was originally added when Italy began exporting it to England, to help preserve the wine during the long ocean voyage. With modern shipping methods, it's no longer necessary, but the bonus booze is still added!

There are two main varieties: sweet Marsala, which is best for making desserts like tiramisu, and dry Marsala, which is amazing for cooking meat, especially chicken and veal.

Leg of Lamb Mediterranean Salad with Red Wine Vinaigrette

Makes 6 to 8 servings

Leg of lamb is another meat that just somehow tastes better when it has been treated to a trip to the grill. With lamb marinated in red wine and more red wine in the salad dressing, this dish is definitely Italian! Check out the way the lamb is prepared for grilling. It's very easy to separate the boned leg into three separate "roasts." They are easier to grill than a butterflied leg, which is thick in some areas and thin in others, so some parts get overcooked. This is one of the longest recipes in the book, but that doesn't mean it's hard. And it's OMG good!

1 boneless leg of lamb
   (about 4 1/2 pounds)

Red Wine and Rosemary Marinade:
1 1/2 cups hearty red wine,
   such as Chianti
1/2 cup extra-virgin olive oil
1/4 cup red wine vinegar
2 tablespoons chopped fresh rosemary, oregano, or mint, or a
   combination
3 garlic cloves, minced
1 teaspoon salt
1/2 teaspoon freshly
   ground black pepper

Red Wine Vinaigrette:
2 tablespoons hearty red wine,
   such as Chianti
2 tablespoons red wine vinegar
1 garlic clove, crushed through
   a press
1/4 teaspoon salt
1/4 teaspoon freshly
   ground black pepper
1/2 cup extra virgin olive oil

Salad:
8 ounces mixed baby greens
1/2 seedless (English) cucumber,
   thinly sliced
1/2 pint (1 cup) grape tomatoes,
   preferably multicolored
1 cup (4 ounces) crumbled feta
   cheese or Italian goat cheese
   (caprino)
1/2 cup pitted and coarsely
   chopped kalamata olives

1. To make the lamb: Discard any string or netting on the lamb. Using a thin, sharp knife, trim away the excess fat from the lamb. Place the lamb, smooth-side down, on the work surface. Following the natural shape of the lamb, cut into three large, fairly equal pieces.

2. To make the marinade: Whisk all of the ingredients together in a medium bowl.

3. Put the lamb in a 1-gallon resealable plastic bag. Pour in the marinade and close the bag. Refrigerate, occasionally turning the bag, for at least 4 and up to 8 hours. Remove the bag from the refrigerator and let stand at room temperature for 30 minutes before grilling the lamb.

4. To make the vinaigrette: Whisk the wine, vinegar, garlic, salt, and pepper together in a small bowl. Gradually whisk in the oil. Cover with plastic wrap and set aside at room temperature for at least 30 minutes and up to 8 hours.

5. Preheat the grill for direct cooking over very high heat (500°F).

6. Remove the lamb from the marinade, shaking off the excess, and discard the marinade. Place the lamb on the cooking grate and close the grill lid. Cook, turning occasionally, with the lid closed as much as possible, until the lamb is well browned and an instant-read thermometer inserted in the center of the lamb reads 130°F for medium-rare, 12 to 15 minutes. Transfer the lamb to a carving board and let stand for 5 minutes.

7. Toss the greens, cucumber, and tomatoes with the vinaigrette in a large bowl. Spread on a very large platter. Sprinkle with the feta and olives.

8. Carve the lamb across the grain on a slight diagonal into thin slices. Arrange in overlapping slices over the salad, drizzle the carving juices on top, and serve immediately.

Mama's Smothered Lamb and Potato Casserole

Makes 6 servings

This is family cooking at its best—the ultimate one-pot, no-fuss dinner, cooked on the grill. Just toss the meat and vegetables together and let it cook so all of the flavors combine. This uses inexpensive shoulder chops that take a while to cook to tenderness, but it's well worth the wait!

¼ cup red wine vinegar

6 lamb shoulder chops
(each about 8 ounces)

4 tablespoons extra-virgin
olive oil, divided

2 teaspoons salt, divided

1 teaspoon freshly ground
black pepper, divided

4 large red-skinned potatoes,
each cut into quarters

3 large carrots,
cut into 1-inch lengths

3 large celery ribs,
cut into 1-inch lengths

2 medium onions,
each cut into quarters

12 garlic cloves, smashed under the
flat side of a knife and peeled

3 tablespoons chopped fresh
flat-leaf parsley, plus more
for serving

½ teaspoon red pepper flakes

½ cup dry white wine

1. Preheat the grill for indirect cooking with medium heat (400°F).

2. Whisk the vinegar with 2 cups water in a large bowl. Add the lamb chops, turn to coat with the vinegar mixture, and let stand for 1 minute. Drain, but do not rinse. Pat the lamb chops dry with paper towels. Brush both sides of the chops with 2 tablespoons of the oil and season with 1 teaspoon salt and ½ teaspoon pepper. Transfer to a baking sheet and set aside.

3. Mix the potatoes, carrots, celery, onions, garlic, parsley, and red pepper flakes together in a large (turkey-size) disposable, aluminum foil roasting pan. Toss with the remaining 2 tablespoons oil and 1 teaspoon salt and ½ teaspoon pepper. Arrange the lamb chops on the vegetable mixture and pour the white wine over all.

4. Place the roasting pan with the lamb on the cooking grate over the unlighted burner(s) and close the lid. Cook for 1½ hours. Remove the lamb chops (you can put them on the grill for a moment), stir the vegetable mixture, and return the lamb to the pan. Continue cooking until the lamb is very tender, about 30 minutes more.

5. Using a slotted spoon, transfer the lamb chops and vegetables to a serving bowl. Skim and discard the fat from the cooking juices in the pan, then pour the juices over the lamb and vegetables. Sprinkle with additional parsley and serve hot.

✳ ✳ ✳ Kitchen ER ✳ ✳ ✳

True story about why outdoor cooking is great: I had a friend of mine make Leg of Lamb Mediterranean Salad for one of his famous dinner parties so I could get some feedback from his guests. In the middle of his party, the kitchen sink sprang a major leak, and plumbers arrived to make an emergency repair. The dinner went on, without a hitch, because the casserole ingredients were ready and waiting in the fridge, and the lamb was cooked and carved outside. And the plumbers loved the leftovers.

✳ ✳ ✳ Vinegar Wash ✳ ✳ ✳

In Italy, they always give lamb a "vinegar wash" before cooking with it to help remove the gamey flavor of farm-raised sheep and to kill any surface bacteria. It's not necessary for those reasons in America today, but we still do it in my house for the flavor.

CHAPTER 6

Pollo (Chicken)

When Italians want to say they know what's going on or
what's really up (especially when it comes to their children), they say,
conosco i miei polli; literally, "I know my chickens."

While it's great to grill big, juicy steaks on the grill, one reason why the Mediterranean diet is healthy is because we don't eat a lot of red meat in Italy. Chicken is our main source of protein, because it's inexpensive and plentiful. In fact, the ancient Romans were believed to be the first Europeans to breed poultry. Today there are more than twenty different breeds raised around Italy.

Chicken does get a bad rap for tending to dry out on the grill, but there are a few things you can do to keep this from happening. You can choose juicier cuts of the chicken, like the thighs; you can cook with the bones in (this is true for all types of meat); or you can just not cook the hell out of it!

People get spooked about chicken being raw on the inside, but heating it to a safe temperature doesn't mean you have to cook it until it's bone-dry. Even the United States Department of Agriculture's (USDA) website recommends using a meat thermometer not only to make sure you've cooked everything to the safe internal temperature, but also "to avoid overcooking" and ruining the flavor of your meal.

USDA Recommended Safe Minimum Internal Temperatures:

Beef, Pork, Lamb, Veal steaks, chops and roasts = 145°F

All other cuts of Beef, Pork, Lamb, Veal = 160°F

All Chicken = 165°F

The USDA's temperatures may be slightly higher than what you prefer. On most meat thermometers, 145° to 160°F is indicated as within the medium-well to well-done range. A lot of chefs instead follow the "traditional" temperatures for doneness. Here they are, as well:

Traditional (Chef) Internal Red Meat Temperatures:

120°F to 130°F = rare

130°F to 135°F = medium-rare

135°F to 145°F = medium

145°F to 150°F = medium-well

150°F to 160°F = well-done

While chicken has a higher internal temperature requirement than other meats, that doesn't mean you have to cook it forever. In some chicken, like that from older birds, the juices won't run clear until after it's been over-cooked, so the only real way to tell you have cooked your chicken correctly is to use a meat thermometer. And then you have to trust it! We've all heard the scary stories about food poisoning, but at 165°F, you're safe. The former Under Secretary for Food Safety, Dr. Richard Raymond, states that at 165°F "consumers can be confident that pathogens and viruses will be destroyed." Getting chicken to that temperature generally takes less than ten minutes on each side with direct cooking. You can also cook chicken over indirect heat just fine—if you want it to look a little browner, you can always move it over a lit burner at the very end.

One of the secrets to juicy boneless chicken breasts is to pound the fillets to an even thickness before cooking them. Put each piece of chicken, one at a time, between two sheets of plastic wrap and lightly pound them using a flat mallet, meat pounder, or a rolling pin until they are about half an inch thick. Notice that I said *lightly* pound. This is not the time to take out your aggression, as chicken is actually more easily torn than steak. And only use a flat pounder—not one of those mean, pointy metal hammers—or else you'll wreck your meal before it's started.

✳ ✳ ✳ Wise Chickens ✳ ✳ ✳

Chicken is a popular subject in Italian cuisine and in our proverbs. There are tons of sayings that have to do with poultry. When you have little kids prowling around your kitchen looking for food, you might say: *I putei se sempre col beco a moia come le galine* or "babies always have their mouths open like chickens!" Health advice? *Per non stare male, va letto con le galline e alzati con il gallo.* "If you don't want to feel bad, go to bed with the chickens and get up with the rooster." The exclamation *Quanne piscia 'a gallina!* is used to mean something will never happen, or that you'll never do something—sort of like "over my dead body" in English. What it literally means in Italian? "When the chicken pees." (Because chickens actually don't pee!)

But my favorite saying of all is *la gallina vecchia fa buon brodo*, which translates to "the old hen makes a good broth," meaning older women are valuable and—I'm not even kidding—good in bed!

Whole Roast Chicken with Herb Rub

Makes 4 to 6 servings

My family loves when I roast a whole chicken on the grill, and I love that it doesn't heat up the house. The crisp brown skin is amazing and so is the tender meat underneath. You can serve the pan sauce on the side, but in Italy, we pour it over the carved bird to make the juiciest chicken you've ever had. If you have a bottle of white wine open, use it to make the sauce, but, really, the drippings are so delicious that you can simply use water. Serve with a big green salad full of lots of vegetables and crusty bread.

Herb Rub:

2 garlic cloves, crushed under the
     flat side of a knife and peeled
¼ teaspoon salt
1 tablespoon extra-virgin olive oil
1 tablespoon dry white wine
1½ teaspoons finely chopped
     fresh thyme
1½ teaspoons finely chopped
     fresh sage or rosemary,
     or a combination
½ teaspoon red pepper flakes

Roast Chicken:

1 (6-pound) roasting chicken, giblets
     reserved, liver discarded or
     saved for another use
2 tablespoons extra-virgin olive oil
1 teaspoon salt
½ teaspoon freshly
     ground black pepper
1 small onion, quartered
½ cup dry white wine, such as
     Pinot Grigio, or water
Fresh sprigs of thyme, rosemary,
     or sage, for garnish

1. To make the rub: Coarsely chop the garlic on a chopping board. Sprinkle with the salt and continue chopping until finely minced. Smear the garlic on the board to make a paste. Transfer to a small bowl and stir in the oil, wine, thyme, sage, and red pepper flakes.

2. To make the chicken: Remove and reserve the pads of yellow fat at the tail. Starting at the tip of the breast, loosen the skin and insert your hand under the skin, loosing the skin all over the chicken as best as you can. Using a small rubber spatula or a dessert spoon, spread the herb rub under the skin and all over the flesh. Rub the chicken all over with the 2 tablespoons oil and season inside and out with salt and pepper. Stuff the onion into the body cavity. Let the chicken stand at room temperature for about 30 minutes.

3. Preheat the grill for indirect cooking with medium heat (400°F).

4. Place the chicken on a wire rack in a metal roasting pan just large enough to hold the chicken. There is no need to truss the chicken. Add the chicken fat and giblet to the roasting pan—they will help flavor the pan juices. Put the roasting pan with the chicken on the grill over the unignited burner(s) and close the lid. Cook, basting quickly with the pan juices every 30 minutes, until an instant-read thermometer inserted in the thickest part of the thigh reads 165°F, about 1¾ hours. Remove the pan from the grill. Stick a large metal spoon into the chicken cavity and tilt it to drain the juices into the roasting pan. Transfer the chicken to a platter. Let the chicken stand for 10 to 15 minutes before carving.

5. Meanwhile, make the pan sauce: Pour the pan juices from the roasting pan into a small glass bowl and let stand 3 minutes. Skim off and discard the yellow fat from the surface. Heat the roasting pan over two stove burners on medium-high heat until the juicy residue in the pan is sizzling, about 30 seconds. (You can also do this on the grill side burner, if you have one.) Pour in the wine and degreased pan juices. Bring the mixture to a boil, scraping up the browned bits in the bottom of the pan with a wooden spoon Boil until reduced by half, about 3 minutes. Remove from the heat.

6. Carve the chicken and arrange on the platter. Pour the pan sauce over the chicken, garnish with the herb sprigs, and serve immediately.

Chicken alla Diavolo

Makes 4 servings

Devilishly hot with red pepper flakes and spicy with garlic, this chicken is always butterflied to expose more of the skin to the heat of the grill so it gets nice and crispy. It's not hard to do with poultry shears or even a sturdy pair of scissors—just wash the scissors well before and after using them for this job. Like the whole chicken, I smear the seasoning under the skin. This is a good way to spread the flavor and also keeps the rub from burning, as it can do when on the outside of the skin.

1 (5-pound) chicken, giblets and liver discarded or saved for another use

6 garlic cloves, smashed under the flat side of a knife and peeled

1 teaspoon salt, divided

5 tablespoons extra-virgin olive oil, divided

1 tablespoon fresh lemon juice

2 teaspoon red pepper flakes

½ teaspoon freshly ground black pepper

1 lemon, cut into wedges, for serving

1. To butterfly the chicken, use poultry shears or a clean pair of scissors, cut through the bones on both sides of the backbone, and discard the backbone. Place the chicken, skin-side up, on a work surface. Press hard on the breast bone that runs vertically between the two breast halves to crack it and spread the chicken. That's it!

2. Coarsely chop the garlic on a chopping board. Sprinkle with ¼ teaspoon of salt and continue chopping until finely minced. Smear the garlic on the board to make a paste. Transfer to a small bowl and stir in 3 tablespoons of oil, the lemon juice, and the red pepper flakes.

3. Remove and discard the pads of yellow fat at the tail. Starting at the tip of the breast, loosen the skin and insert your hand under the skin, loosing the skin all over the chicken as best as you can. Using a small rubber spatula or a dessert spoon, spread the red pepper rub under the skin and all over the flesh. Brush the chicken with the remaining 2 tablespoons of oil on both sides and season all over with the remaining ¾ teaspoon salt and the pepper. Let stand at room temperature while preparing the grill.

4. Preheat the grill for indirect cooking with medium-high heat (450°F).

5. Place the chicken on the cooking grate, skin-side down, over the unignited burner(s), and close the grill lid. Cook until the skin is golden brown, about 40 minutes. (Do not move the chicken because the skin will stick to the grate if moved too soon.) Flip the chicken and continue cooking, with the lid closed, until the skin is crisp and brown and an instant-read thermometer inserted in the thickest part of the thigh reads 165°F, 20 to 30 minutes more. If you wish, move the chicken to the heated side of the grill, skin-side down, and continue cooking to crisp the skin a bit more, about 3 minutes. Transfer the chicken to a carving board and let stand for 10 minutes.

6. Cut the chicken into serving pieces and transfer to a platter. Add the lemon wedges, and serve hot.

Pollo (Chicken)

Marinated Chicken Breasts
with Grilled Apple Rings

Makes 6 servings

We talked about how great pork tastes with apple flavoring, and the same is true of chicken. (In fact, you can use the apple-rosemary marinade with pork, as well.) This is one of my favorite grilled recipes.

Apple-Rosemary Marinade:

3/4 cup apple cider or apple juice

3/4 cup dry white wine, such as
   Pinot Grigio

1/2 cup coarsely chopped onion

1/4 cup extra-virgin olive oil

1 1/2 tablespoons finely chopped
   fresh rosemary

1 1/2 teaspoons salt

1 1/2 teaspoons freshly ground
   black pepper

Chicken Breast:

3 Red Delicious or Golden
   Delicious apples, washed
   but unpeeled, cored, and cut
   into 1/2-inch rings

6 skinless boneless chicken breast
   halves (each 6 ounces)

1. To make the marinade: Whisk the apple cider, wine, onion, oil, rosemary, salt, and pepper together in a medium bowl.

2. Place the apple rings in a 1-quart resealable plastic bag. Pour in about 1/3 cup of the marinade (including the onion and rosemary), and close the bag. Set aside.

3. To make the chicken: One at a time, place a chicken breast half between 2 plastic storage bags. Using a flat meat pounder or a rolling pin, pound the chicken until it is about 1/2-inch thick. Place the chicken breast halves in a 1-gallon resealable plastic bag. Add the remaining marinade and close the bag. Refrigerate the bags of chicken and apple, turning occasionally, for 1 to 2 hours.

4. Remove the chicken and apples from the marinade, transfer to a plate, and discard the marinade. Let the chicken and apples stand at room temperature while preheating the grill.

5. Preheat the grill for direct heating over medium heat (400°F).

6. Place the chicken on the cooking grate and close the lid. Cook until the undersides are seared with grill marks, about 4 minutes. Flip the chicken over and cook, with the lid closed as much as possible, until it feels firm when pressed with your finger, 4 to 6 minutes more. Transfer to a platter and tent with aluminum foil to keep warm. Add the apples to the grill and cook, with the lid closed, flipping once, until seared with grill marks and crisp-tender, 4 to 5 minutes total. Add the apples to the platter with the chicken. Serve hot.

✱ ✱ ✱ My Shy Little Star ✱ ✱ ✱

hear all the time from fans that you all want to see more of Gabriella. She isn't shy by normal standards, but I guess compared to her over-the-top sisters, she is. She is outspoken and sweet and creative and wonderful, but she doesn't love the cameras in our house, so she generally runs from them. We don't want to force her to perform or do anything, so we let her be. But believe me, as soon as they leave, she emerges! She loves to meet people though and comes with me to book signings sometimes—she even signs her name!—so stop by and see me when I come to your area, and maybe you'll get to meet Miss Gabriella in person.

Chicken Breasts Stuffed with Artichokes and Fontina

Makes 6 servings

I love making fancy dishes on the grill that seem like they can only be made inside. Like stuffing a chicken breast with artichokes (my fave!) and fontina cheese. This is a great dish for when you have company. Just be careful not to overmarinate the chicken, or it will get tough from the acid in the artichoke marinade and the wine.

Basil-Rosemary Marinade:
1 (6-ounce) jar marinated
    artichoke hearts
¼ cup dry white wine,
    such as Pinot Grigio
¼ cup extra-virgin olive oil
1 tablespoon finely chopped
    fresh basil
2 teaspoons finely chopped
    fresh rosemary
2 garlic cloves, minced
1 teaspoon salt
½ teaspoon freshly ground
    black pepper

Chicken Breasts:
6 boneless skinless chicken breast
    halves (each 6 ounces)
½ cup (2 ounces) shredded
    fontina cheese

1. To make the marinade: Drain the artichokes hearts, reserving the marinade from the jar. Set the artichoke hearts aside. Whisk the wine, oil, reserved artichoke marinade, basil, rosemary, garlic, salt, and pepper together in a medium bowl.

2. To make the chicken: Working with one chicken breast half at a time, use a thin sharp knife to cut horizontally through the center of the chicken, cutting almost, but not quite, to the other side. Transfer the chicken to a 1-gallon resealable plastic bag. Add the marinade and close the bag. Refrigerate, occasionally turning the bag, for 1 to 2 hours.

3. Coarsely chop the reserved artichoke hearts. Transfer to a bowl and combine with the fontina cheese. Remove the chicken from the marinade, discarding the marinade. Open up a chicken breast half like a book. Place about one-sixth of the artichoke mixture on one side of the chicken, and close to cover with the other half. Repeat with the remaining chicken breasts and artichoke mixture. Let stand at room temperature while preparing the grill.

4. Preheat the grill for direct cooking over medium heat (400°F).

5. Place the chicken breasts on the cooking grate and close the grill lid. Cook until the undersides are golden brown and seared with grill marks, about 5 minutes. Carefully flip the chicken (the filling will stay in place) and continue cooking, with the lid closed, until the chicken feels firm when pressed on top with a fingertip, 6 to 8 minutes more. Remove the chicken breasts from the grill. Let the chicken stand for 5 minutes, then serve hot.

✳ ✳ ✳ One Fabulicious, Non-grilled Side ✳ ✳ ✳

I love cooking on the grill, but sometimes the amount of food you're cooking or the amount of people you're cooking for (especially if you have someone in your life like my husband who could easily bring home an entire town for dinner unannounced) doesn't match up with the size of your grill. Or maybe sometimes you just want to concentrate all of your grilling energy on the meaty main course. Then there are those times when you have a "helpful" friend or relative over who insists on cooking, too … For these situations, I'm giving you one very special non-grilled dish. It's fast, fabulicious, and features my Fabellini sparkling wine as a glaze for carrots (page 174). *Salute!*

Gabriella's Grilled Chicken Parmesan

Makes 6 servings

One of the recipes from *Fabulicious! Teresa's Italian Family Cookbook* that I get complimented on the most is Gabriella's favorite meal: Chicken Parmigiana. It's hard to believe you can make such a succulent layered dish on the grill, but you can, and it's just as fantastic as the original oven version.

6 skinless boneless chicken breast halves (each about 6 ounces)

2 tablespoons extra-virgin olive oil

1 teaspoon salt

½ teaspoon freshly ground black pepper

¾ cup Italian-seasoned dry bread crumbs

⅓ cup (about 1½ ounces) freshly grated Parmesan cheese

1 cup (4 ounces) shredded fresh mozzarella cheese

3 cups "The Quickie" Tomato Sauce (page 56)

1. One at a time, place half a chicken breast between 2 plastic storage bags. Using a flat meat pounder or a rolling pin, pound the chicken until it is about ½-inch thick. Brush the chicken on both sides with the oil, and season with the salt and black pepper.

2. Mix the bread crumbs and Parmesan cheese together on a plate. Dip and coat the chicken on both sides in the breadcrumb mixture, patting the coating to help it adhere. Transfer to a baking sheet. Let stand at room temperature while preparing the grill.

3. Preheat the grill for direct cooking over medium heat (400°F).

4. Using a wad of paper towels dipped in olive oil, wipe the cooking grate to grease it. Place the chicken on the grate and close the lid. Cook until the coating on the underside is golden brown and seared with grill marks, about 4 minutes. Carefully flip the chicken and continue cooking, with the lid closed, until the chicken feels firm when pressed on top with a fingertip, about 4 minutes more. During the last minute, top each chicken breast half with mozzarella. Transfer the chicken to a platter.

5. For each serving, spoon ½ cup of the tomato sauce on a dinner plate and top with a chicken breast half. Serve hot.

Juicy Joe's Chicken and Broccoli Rabe Dinner

Makes 6 servings

This is Joe's specialty. He loves broccoli rabe—we all do!—and he makes this for us all the time. It's super simple but so delicious! I usually serve this with plain ziti to help mellow out the broccoli's bite.

6 skinless boneless chicken breast halves (each about 6 ounces)

3 tablespoons extra-virgin olive oil, divided

Salt and freshly ground black pepper

1 pound broccoli rabe, well washed

1 large onion, chopped

5 garlic cloves, crushed under the flat side of a knife and peeled

1. Preheat the grill for direct cooking over medium heat (400°F). One at a time, place half of a chicken breast between 2 plastic storage bags. Using a flat meat pounder or a rolling pin, pound the chicken until it is about ½-inch thick. Brush the chicken on both sides with 2 tablespoons of oil and season with 1 teaspoon salt and ½ teaspoon pepper. Let stand at room temperature for 15 to 30 minutes.

2. Meanwhile, bring a large saucepan of lightly salted water to a boil over high heat. Add the broccoli rabe and cook until crisp-tender, about 5 minutes. Drain well.

3. Place the chicken breast halves on the cooking grate and close the grill lid. Cook until the undersides are seared with grill marks, about 4 minutes. Flip the chicken over and continue cooking, with the lid closed, until the chicken feels firm when pressed on top with a fingertip, 4 to 6 minutes more. Remove the chicken breasts from the heat and transfer to a chopping board. Let stand while finishing the broccoli rabe.

Teresa's Tip

Get the Italian-seasoned dry bread crumbs, but not the cheese-flavored kind. If you want cheese, you can always mix in freshly grated Parmesan. The "cheese" they include in the breadcrumb can is not … well … fresh. Or even really cheese.

4. Heat the remaining tablespoon of oil in a large skillet over medium heat. Add the onion and cook, stirring occasionally, until translucent, about 5 minutes. Stir in the broccoli rabe and garlic. Cook until the broccoli rabe is tender, about 5 minutes. Season with salt and pepper.

5. Cut the chicken across the grain into $1/2$-inch-thick slices. Transfer the chicken slices and juices to the skillet and cook to blend the flavors, about 2 minutes. Remove the garlic cloves and serve hot.

Chicken Thighs with Sweet and Spicy Rub

Makes 6 servings

I prefer firm and tender white chicken meat, but Joe and my kids love the juicy dark meat. And while I peel off the skin, I know some of you love it, especially when it's crispy! (Even I splurge every once in awhile, and the skin on this is *fabulicious*!) So here is a recipe with lots of options. I put the rub under the skin directly onto the chicken so if you do like to eat it skinless, you won't be pulling off all of the flavor with the skin.

Sweet and Spicy Rub:
1 tablespoon light brown sugar
2 teaspoons salt
2 teaspoons sweet paprika,
   preferably smoked paprika
2 teaspoons dried thyme
1 teaspoon garlic powder
1 teaspoon onion powder
1 teaspoon freshly ground
   black pepper

Chicken Thighs:
12 chicken thighs with skin
   and bone
Extra-virgin olive oil

1. To make the rub: Mix all of the ingredients together in a small bowl.

2. To make the chicken: Separate the skin from each thigh, leaving it attached on one side. Sprinkle the rub all over the chicken flesh, and pull the skin back into place. Brush on both sides with oil. Let stand at room temperature while preparing the grill.

3. Preheat the grill for indirect cooking with medium-high heat (450°F).

4. Put the chicken on the cooking grate over the unignited burner(s), skin side down, and close the grill lid. Cook until the skin is golden brown, about 30 minutes. Flip the chicken and continue cooking, with the lid closed, until it shows no sign of pink when pierced at the bone with the tip of a small knife, about 15 minutes more. (The chicken thighs are too thin to get an accurate reading on a meat thermometer.) Remove from the grill. Serve hot, with or without the skin.

Chicken Spiedini with Basil Glaze

Makes 6 servings

Skewers are great for serving guests because you can personalize them to suit anyone; and they're super easy. I sometimes use zucchini or mushroom caps instead of the peppers and onions.

Special equipment:
6 metal grilling skewers

Basil Glaze:
2 garlic cloves, crushed under the
    flat side of a knife and peeled
1 cup packed fresh basil leaves
½ cup extra-virgin olive oil
Salt and freshly ground
    black pepper

Spiedini:
2 pounds skinless boneless chicken
    breast, cut into 24 pieces
1 small red bell pepper, cored and
    cut into 12 pieces
1 small yellow or green bell pepper,
    cored and cut into 12 pieces
½ medium red onion, separated
    into layers and cut into 12 large
    chunks (small pieces discarded
    or saved for another use)
Extra-virgin olive oil
½ teaspoon salt
½ teaspoon freshly ground
    black pepper
½ cup (2 ounces) freshly grated
    Parmesan cheese, for serving

1. To make the glaze: With the machine on high, drop the garlic through the feed tube of a food processor until minced. Add the basil leaves and process until chopped. With the machine still running, gradually add the oil. Season with salt and pepper. (Or process all of the ingredients in a blender to make a thin paste.)

2. To make the spiedini: For each serving, thread 6 pieces of chicken, and 2 each of red and yellow peppers and red onions onto a metal skewer. (Do not pack them closely.) Brush the skewers with oil and season with the salt and pepper. Let stand at room temperature while preparing the grill.

3. Preheat the grill for direct cooking over medium heat (400°F).

4. Place the spiedini on the grate and close the grill lid. Grill until the undersides of the chicken are seared with grill marks, about 5 minutes. Turn the spiedini and continue cooking, with the lid closed, until the chicken feels firm when pressed on top with a fingertip and the vegetables are crisp-tender, about 5 minutes more. During the last 2 minutes, brush the spiedini generously with the basil glaze and turn occasionally to set the glaze. Transfer the skewers to a platter.

5. Sprinkle the chicken and vegetables with the Parmesan cheese. Serve hot.

CHAPTER 7

Pesce (Seafood)

In Italy, instead of saying "the early bird gets the worm" (because who really wants a worm?), we turn it around and warn you against staying in bed and being lazy by saying *chi dorme non piglia pesci* or "he who sleeps doesn't catch any fish." And we all want the fish!

W̲e spend our entire summer, every single moment we can, at the Jersey Shore. Whether at our own house or visiting friends' houses, we do almost of all our cooking outdoors. Everyone either has a huge patio or dock—some on the ocean, some on the bay—and everybody has a grill.

The great thing about being so close to the water is that we can get fresh seafood almost all the time. Joe has a couple of crab traps that he baits with pieces of chicken or bunker, then throws over the side of our dock in the morning. By nighttime, we're feasting on fresh crab.

I think a lot of Italians settled in New Jersey because it is so close to the water. No matter where you are in New Jersey, you're always less than 70 miles from the beach. Italy is only 100 miles wide at its widest point (not counting that top bit bordering Europe), so we're used to having easy access to the ocean.

I've been cleaning and cooking seafood my whole life. Because it can be so easy to get (and pulling it out of the ocean means it's free!) and so quick to cook, it's what my mom usually served at big parties. I remember growing up, we'd have thirty-five people over like it was nothing. I loved helping my mom prepare all the food, especially the seafood! My favorite is sea bass; I love how flaky, buttery, and soft it is. And I've already confessed my love of octopus. There's really not a kind of seafood that I *don't* like. Anchovies, baccalà . . . bring it on! But don't worry, I'm going to give you my most delicious seafood recipes that star everybody's favorite fish: sea bass, swordfish, tuna steaks, and even salmon stuffed with crab.

MINDING NEMO

Now I know I've been saying that you have to be careful with the high heat when grilling, but that doesn't apply to seafood. Seafood is especially delicate, so that doesn't make sense at first, but let me explain. If you overcook seafood, it's just no good. And since it's delicate, it's very vulnerable to being overcooked. The best way to protect it inside is to get a nice crust on the outside.

Fish meat is flaky, which also means it falls apart much, much easier than chicken or steak. The best way to stop it from sticking to the grill (and leaving clumps behind when you try and flip it) is to be sure that the cooking grate is super clean, so give it a really good scrub with the grill brush. If you grill a lot of fish, get a perforated grill pan to put on the cooking grate because, unlike the grate, you can wash it well between uses. Another trick is to always lightly, but thoroughly, oil the fish.

Once you put your fish on the grill, don't touch it. Don't move it, don't shift it, don't stick your spatula under it to try and loosen it. Instead, let it cook, with the lid closed, over high heat until a thin, golden exterior crust forms on the underside, usually two or three minutes. At that point, the fish will let go of the grill, and you can flip it in one beautiful piece. So don't touch it for a few minutes, until you're sure the crust has formed.

Crab-Stuffed Salmon Involtini

Makes 6 servings

Involtini, "rolls" in Italian, is when you wrap a thin piece of meat, usually veal, pork, or seafood, around a stuffing. I love to use easy-to-roll salmon stuffed with crab. Since the salmon has been butterflied, it won't take long to cook. Depending on the price of seafood in your area, this recipe can be kind of a splurge, so you might want to save it for when you have company or a celebration.

Stuffing:

1 cup crabmeat, picked over
   for cartilage and shells
1 scallion, white and green parts,
   finely chopped
2 tablespoons mayonnaise
1 tablespoon fresh lemon juice
1 tablespoon Italian-seasoned
   dry bread crumbs
½ teaspoon Worcestershire sauce
Salt
Hot red pepper sauce,
   such as Tabasco

Salmon:

6 skinless salmon fillets (each about
   6 ounces)
Extra-virgin olive oil, for brushing
½ teaspoon salt
½ teaspoon freshly
   ground black pepper
Lemon wedges, for serving

1. Preheat the grill for direct cooking over high heat (500°F).

2. To make the stuffing: Mix the crabmeat, scallion, mayonnaise, lemon juice, bread crumbs, and Worcestershire in a medium bowl. Season with salt and hot pepper sauce.

3. To make the salmon: Place a salmon fillet with the short end facing you. Using a sharp knife, cut the fillet horizontally through its center, reaching almost, but not quite, to the other side. Open up the fillet like a book. Spread one-sixth of the stuffing on one side of the fillet and close the fillet. Repeat with the remaining fillets and stuffing. Lightly brush the fillets on both sides with oil and season with the salt and pepper.

4. Place the fillets on the cooking grate and close the grill lid. Cook, without moving the fillets, until the undersides are seared with grill marks, about 2 minutes. Carefully flip the fillets (the filling will stay in place), and continue cooking, with the lid closed as much as possible, just until is the other side seared with grill marks and the salmon looks opaque with a hint of rosy pink when flaked in the center with the tip of a sharp knife, about 2 minutes more. Remove the salmon from the grill. Serve hot with the lemon wedges.

Grilled Sea Bass with Lemon-Wine Sauce and Pistachios

Makes 6 servings

Wanna know a secret about the delicious creamy lemon-wine sauce that upscale restaurants serve with seafood? It's easy and inexpensive to make at home—and it's not even made with cream! It's actually butter that's very slowly heated until it looks creamy. Make the sauce just before you put the fish on the grill, and keep it warm by placing the saucepan in a skillet of hot, but not simmering water.

Lemon-Wine Sauce:

1 tablespoon extra-virgin olive oil

2 tablespoons minced shallot

1 cup dry white wine,
    such as Pinot Grigio

2 tablespoons white wine vinegar

Finely grated zest of 1 lemon

2 tablespoons fresh lemon juice

1 cup (2 sticks) cold unsalted
    butter, cut into tablespoons

Salt and freshly ground
    black pepper

Sea Bass:

6 skinless sea bass fillets
    (each about 6 ounces)

Extra-virgin olive oil, for brushing

1/2 teaspoon salt

1/2 teaspoon freshly ground
    black pepper

1/3 cup coarsely chopped
    pistachios

1. To make the sauce: Heat the oil in a medium saucepan over medium heat. Add the shallots and cook, stirring occasionally, until softened, about 2 minutes. Add the wine, vinegar, lemon zest, and juice. Bring to a boil over high heat and cook until reduced to about 2 tablespoons, 5 to 7 minutes. Reduce the heat to its lowest setting.

2. One tablespoon at a time, whisk the butter into the shallot mixture, whisking constantly until each addition softens before adding the next. The butter should warm and soften into a creamy sauce, and not actually melt. If the butter looks melted, remove the saucepan from the heat and immediately whisk in another tablespoon of cold butter. It should take about 2 minutes to add all of the butter. Season with salt and pepper. Remove from the heat. (At this point, you may strain out the shallots and lemon zest through a wire sieve into a small bowl, but it won't do any harm to leave them in for a slightly less smooth sauce.) Put the saucepan (or bowl) in a skillet of very hot water over very low heat to keep the sauce warm for up to 1 hour. The sauce should be warm, not piping hot, and it will warm up when it comes into contact with the hot fish.

3. Preheat the grill for direct cooking over high heat (500°F).

4. To make the sea bass: Lightly oil the sea bass fillets on both sides with the oil and season with the salt and pepper. Place on the cooking grate and close the grill lid. Cook until the undersides are seared with grill marks, about 3 minutes. Flip the fillets and continue cooking, with the lid closed, until the flesh in the center looks barely opaque when flaked with the tip of a small sharp knife, about 3 minutes more. Remove the fillets from the grill.

5. To serve, place a sea bass fillet on each of six dinner plates, and top each with 2 tablespoons of the sauce. Sprinkle with the pistachios and serve hot.

Teresa's Tip

Any leftover lemon-wine sauce—or double the recipe so you have extra—can be refrigerated in an airtight container for up to 2 days. When you're ready to use it again, bring it to room temperature before using as a sauce for steamed or boiled vegetables.

Tuna Steaks with Pepper-Olive Relish

Makes 6 servings

Especially when cooked perfectly rare, juicy tuna steaks are just as delicious as a tender beef steak—and much healthier! For the best outcome, get sushi-grade tuna from a first-class fish store. You can cook it beyond medium-rare, but if you do, just don't expect it to be very moist. This pepper-olive relish is not only amazing with the tuna, but you'll also find it works well with pork chops or salmon, on burgers, or even on bruschetta.

Pepper-Olive Relish:

2 red bell peppers, roasted and skinned (see Grilling Peppers, page 178), cut into 1/2-inch dice

1/3 cup coarsely chopped pitted Kalamata olives

1 tablespoon fresh lemon juice

1 tablespoon finely chopped fresh oregano or basil

1 garlic clove, minced

Salt and red pepper flakes

Tuna Steaks:

6 tuna steaks (each 6 ounces and cut 1 inch thick)

Extra-virgin olive oil

1 teaspoon salt

1/2 teaspoon freshly ground black pepper

1. To make the relish: Mix the roasted peppers, olives, lemon juice, oregano, and garlic together in a small bowl. Season with salt and red pepper flakes. Cover and let stand at room temperature for at least 30 minutes so that the flavors can blend. (The relish can be made in advance and stored in the refrigerator for up to 3 days. Bring to room temperature before serving.)

2. Preheat the grill for direct cooking over high heat (500°F).

3. To make the tuna steaks: Lightly brush the tuna on both sides with oil and season with the salt and pepper. Place the tuna on the cooking grate and cook until the undersides are seared with grill marks, about 2 1/2 minutes. Flip the tuna and continue cooking, with the lid closed, until the other sides are seared and the tuna is opaque on the outside with a rosy pink center when cut with a small sharp knife, about 2 1/2 minutes more.

4. Place a tuna steak on each of six dinner plates, and top with equal amounts of the relish. Serve hot.

Swordfish with Cherry Tomato–Caper Salsa

Makes 6 servings

This tomato-caper salsa goes great with any "strong" fish—such as tuna and swordfish—or "meaty" white fish—such as halibut or this swordfish. You can use grape tomatoes instead, but summer farm stand cherry tomatoes (especially the pretty, multicolored ones) give the dish extra color.

Cherry Tomato–Caper Salsa:

1 pint cherry tomatoes, cut in halves

3 tablespoons finely chopped
   red onion

2 tablespoons extra-virgin olive oil

2 tablespoons white
   or red wine vinegar

2 tablespoons drained and rinsed
   capers, coarsely chopped if large

1 tablespoon finely chopped
   fresh basil

1 tablespoon finely chopped
   fresh flat-leaf parsley

1 garlic clove, minced

Salt and freshly ground
   black pepper

Swordfish:

6 swordfish steaks (each about
   6 ounces and cut about
   1 inch thick)

Extra-virgin olive oil, for brushing

1/2 teaspoon salt

1/2 teaspoon freshly ground
   black pepper

1. To make the salsa: Mix the the cherry tomatoes, red onion, olive oil, vinegar, capers, basil, parsley, and garlic in a small bowl together in a small bowl. Season with salt and pepper. Cover and let stand at room temperature for at least 30 minutes and up to 4 hours to allow the flavors to blend.

2. Preheat the grill for direct cooking over high heat (500°F).

3. To make the swordfish: Lightly brush the swordfish on both sides with oil and season with the salt and pepper. Place the swordfish on the cooking grate and close the grill lid. Cook until the undersides are seared with grill marks, about 3 minutes. Flip the swordfish and continue cooking, with the lid closed, until the other sides are seared and the swordfish is just opaque to the center when cut with a small sharp knife, 3 to 4 minutes more. Remove from the grill.

4. Place a swordfish steak on each of six dinner plates, and top with equal amounts of the salsa. Serve hot.

✳ ✳ ✳ With Love From Capri ✳ ✳ ✳

Although they're most famously used in veal or chicken piccata dishes, capers also go well with seafood because their saltiness is a great complement to the fish. Capers are actually the pickled and pre-served flower buds of a caper bush, which grows along the coast of Italy and was named for the island of Capri (along with those cute, cropped summer pants). The plant is very delicate, and the buds can only be picked by hand, which is why the little jars of capers you see in the supermarket are so expensive—but so worth it!

When the flower buds are allowed to grow, bloom, and turn into a fruit, those can also be harvested and pickled, and are later served as caperberries (great for an antipasti platter!).

Capers have been flavoring dishes for thousands of years and are believed by some to be an aphrodisiac. King Solomon even talks about them in the Bible as a cause of sexual desire. No joke. Ecclesiastes 12:5. Look it up!

Clams with Lemon-Caper Butter

Make 4 servings

If you've ever been to an Italian cookout, you've probably seen a few large, disposable aluminum pans on the grill. We use those for cooking wet things that we want to mix and mingle, like clams and this yummy lemon-caper butter sauce. You can use littleneck or cherrystone clams—just know the larger cherrystones take a little longer to cook.

48 littleneck clams

¼ cup extra-virgin olive oil

4 tablespoons (½ stick)
   unsalted butter

6 garlic cloves, minced

¾ cup dry white wine, such as
   Pinot Grigio

¼ cup fresh lemon juice

2 tablespoons drained and rinsed
   capers, coarsely chopped if large

2 tablespoons finely chopped
   fresh flat-leaf parsley

Lemon wedges, for serving

Hot red pepper sauce, for serving

1. Scrub the clams well under cold running water. Transfer to a big bowl or pot and add enough cold salted ice water to cover. (How much salt? The water should taste salty, but not as strong as sea water.) Let stand for 1 to 2 hours. Drain well.

2. Preheat the grill for direct cooking over medium heat (400°F).

3. Place a large disposable aluminum foil roasting pan on the cooking grate. Add the oil, butter, and garlic and cook, stirring often, until the butter is melted and the garlic is fragrant and softened, about 3 minutes. Stir in the wine, lemon juice, capers, and parsley. Add the clams and close the grill lid.

4. Cook, occasionally shaking the pan, until the clams have opened, 10 to 15 minutes. Discard any unopened clams. Remove the pan from the grill. Using tongs, divide the clams among four deep bowls, and top with equal amounts of the cooking liquid. Serve hot with the lemon wedges and hot pepper sauce.

* * * The No-Cheese-on-Fish "Rule" * * *

Some Italians and Italian-Americans act like putting any kind of cheese on any kind of fish is completely taboo. It's really not. I get that you don't want to drown out the subtle flavors of seafood with sharp-tasting cheese, but a tiny sprinkling isn't going to overpower anything. In fact, I think it can enhance the flavors of some seafood.

So where did this "rule" come from? No one really knows. It doesn't seem to be for religious reasons, since even though the Catholic Church used to rule no meat *or* dairy on Fridays, we had no problem putting cheese on nonseafood meat the other days of the week. And while some Italian grandmas used to say any milk product with fish would "make you sick," that's not true. Maybe back before refrigeration, there was a concern that the strong taste of cheese could "hide" the taste of spoiled fish, and you could get sick from that, but that's hardly the case any more.

More likely, it has to do with simple geography. For the most part, people in the regions of Italy that fish didn't have cows for milk, and the cattle farms that were landlocked didn't have fresh fish. I'm not sure it was really a rule as much as the people who fished a lot just didn't have cheese.

Even today, there isn't the same availability of ingredients in Italy as there is in America. One of my friends was in Tuscany recently, and his hosts were making a big deal out of how their family in Sicily was FedEx-ing some fresh mozzarella to them. Here, we would just walk into Whole Foods and buy it.

So feel free to put cheese on your fish. (In a respectful way of course. Don't go all "Olive Garden" on me!) You're not really breaking any rules, you won't get your "honorary Italian" status revoked, and if anyone gives you any grief, you can send 'em my way!

Parmesan-Crusted Scallop Spiedini

Makes 4 servings

I know, I know—I've heard all the Italian-American chefs say the same thing: never, ever put cheese on seafood. Here's the deal: I'm not a chef. I am a true Italian though, and I promise you, this is worth breaking the rules for! The sharp Parmesan is amazing paired with the mellow scallops. Try to get the big "dry" scallops, which weigh about 1-ounce each. Also, to keep the bread-crumb coating from burning, the grill temperature should be medium (around 400°F)—not as high as we use for other seafood recipes. The scallops are skewered to help to turn them, but these are not "kebabs" in the traditional sense, with vegetables included with the seafood.

Special Equipment:
4 metal grilling skewers

16 large scallops, preferably dry, about 1 ounce each
2 tablespoons extra-virgin olive oil, plus more for drizzling on the scallops and greasing the grate
1/2 teaspoon salt
1/2 teaspoon freshly ground black pepper
1/3 cup plain dry bread crumbs
2 tablespoons freshly grated Parmesan cheese
2 tablespoons finely chopped fresh flat-leaf parsley
2 garlic cloves, minced
Lemon wedges, for serving

1. Lightly brush the scallops all over with oil and season with the salt and pepper.

2. Mix ix the bread crumbs, Parmesan cheese, parsley, garlic, and 2 tablespoons of oil in a medium bowl. In batches, add the scallops and turn to coat completely in the breadcrumb mixture. Thread 4 scallops on each of 4 metal grilling skewers. Place the skewers on a plate and refrigerate to set the coating for 30 minutes.

3. Preheat the grill for direct cooking over medium heat (400°F).

4. Lightly oil the cooking grate. Drizzle a little more oil over the scallops. Place the scallops directly on the grill and close the lid. Cook, turning occasionally, with the lid closed as much as possible, until the coating is golden brown and the scallops are opaque and feel firm when pressed with a fingertip, about 8 minutes. Remove the scallops from the grill. Slide the scallops off the skewers and serve hot with the lemon wedges.

Shrimp Skewers with Salsa Verde

Makes 6 servings

Salsa verde is a green sauce similar to pesto: it's uncooked, made from herbs (in this case, parsley instead of basil), and can be served with about a zillion different foods. For example, add chunks of bell peppers to the skewers, if you wish. For this recipe, the thin, inexpensive skewers sold at most supermarkets work better than the flat-bladed metal "kebab" variety.

Special equipment:
8 thin metal grilling skewers

Salsa Verde:
1½ cups packed fresh
    flat-leaf parsley
1 scallion, white and green parts,
    coarsely chopped
Finely grated zest of 1 lemon
¼ cup fresh lemon juice
¼ cup drained and rinsed capers
1½ teaspoons anchovy paste
2 garlic cloves, crushed under the
    flat side of a knife and peeled
½ cup extra virgin olive oil
Salt and freshly ground
    black pepper

Shrimp Skewers:
36 jumbo (21 to 26 count) shrimp,
    peeled and deveined
2 tablespoons extra-virgin olive oil
¼ teaspoon salt
¼ teaspoon freshly ground
    black pepper

1. To make the salsa: Process the parsley, scallion, lemon zest and juice, capers, anchovy paste, and garlic in a food processor or blender until coarsely chopped. With the machine running, gradually pour in the oil to make a rough-textured sauce. Season with salt and pepper. Transfer to a medium bowl and cover. Let stand at room temperature for 1 to 2 hours to allow the flavors to blend. (The salsa verde can be refrigerated for up to 3 days. Bring to room temperature before using.)

2. Preheat the grill for direct cooking over high heat (500°F).

3. To make the shrimp skewers: Have ready 8 thin metal skewers ready. Toss the shrimp, oil, salt, and pepper together in a large bowl to coat. Hold 2 metal skewers parallel to each other. Curving the shrimp into its natural "C" shape, thread the shrimp onto the skewers, leaving a little room between the shrimp. (The exact number of shrimp per skewer isn't important.)

4. Place the skewered shrimp on the cooking grate and close the grill lid. Grill until the edges of the shrimp look opaque, about 2 minutes. Turn the skewers and continue cooking, with the lid closed, until they are completely opaque and feel firm when pressed with a fingertip, about 2 minutes more. Remove the skewers from the grill and slide the shrimp off the skewers.

5. Spoon about 3 tablespoons of the salsa verde onto each of six dinner plates. Top each with 6 shrimp. Serve hot.

Teresa's Tip

It's easier to grill shrimp if they are skewered. To keep them from spinning on the skewer, thread them side-by-side onto two skewers, and they'll stay put.

---

* * * Spicy Salsa * * *

When most people hear the world salsa, they think of the spicy dip made from chopped veggies and eaten with tortilla chips. But salsa actually means the same thing in both Spanish and Italian: "sauce." Unlike the American definition of "sauce" as a thin liquid, Italian and Spanish salsa is deliciously chunky and raw. It's an easy accompaniment for almost any dish, and while the Italian version isn't necessarily spicy, you can always heat it up by adding a couple of minced pepperoncini.

CHAPTER 8

Pasta

Esse nufesso qui dice male di macaroni.

"One has to be an idiot to speak badly of pasta."

IN o matter how we cook our food, pasta is still an essential part of the Italian meal. While Americans eat about twenty pounds of pasta per person a year, Italians beat that three times over, eating more than sixty pounds. And yet, the Italian people are not three times fatter. In fact, it's the opposite. Worldwide obesity rates from 2010 show that America has the second highest obesity rate in the world with twenty-eight percent of all adults being medically classified as obese, while Italy has one of the smallest percentages, at just ten percent. Clearly pasta is not the problem. (What a relief, right? Since pasta is so, so good!)

Here's why I think pasta can be such a huge part of the Mediterranean diet and the Italian people can still stay skinny: because instead of eating deep-fried, white-flour, sugar-covered foods, we fill up on pasta. And while people in American often put pasta and bread in the same "bad carbs" category, they actually aren't the same. Pasta isn't made from the same white flour you make bread or cupcakes with. Even the regular "white" pasta is made from durum wheat—a hard, coarse wheat naturally high in protein. (Use the whole grain pasta, and that's even healthier!)

We also don't traditionally cover our pasta in crazy, buttery, melty, cheesy sauces; we toss it in extra virgin oil and sprinkle just a bit of a sharp-tasting fresh cheese over the top for flavor. Instead of a staple, super creamy sauces are considered a big treat. And we don't just eat a giant plate of pasta with sauce and call it a day. We use pasta as a sort of vehicle for carrying other foods—mostly vegetables—into the body. Meat can accompany pasta, but it isn't the majority of our plate.

So just because we're grilling up seasonal vegetables and a lot of lean meats, we don't abandon our precious pasta. It takes just a few minutes to cook up noodles *al dente* in a pot of salted water. On my grill, because I have extra side burners and an outdoor sink for draining the pasta water, I do it outside next to the grill, so I don't even have to keep going back and forth between the grill and my kitchen.

✳ ✳ ✳ I Heart Side Burners ✳ ✳ ✳

I know I said you don't need a million extras on your grill, and you don't, but there is one that I have and can't live without: stove-like burners on the side. Here's why: when cooking a lot of food for a lot of people, timing is everything. I don't want people waiting thirty minutes between courses. I don't want the main course to get cold while I'm still cooking the sides. In an ideal world, everything gets done at the same time. The extra burners right there on the grill can help make that happen.

I bring a pan from kitchen and sauté the garlic and onions on a side burner while I'm preheating the grill. I use a small pot to boil water and cook the pasta right next to the sizzling ingredients that I'll toss into it. It's not a necessity, but if you can afford it, side burners are well worth the extra price.

POTS AND PANS ON THE GRILL

Don't feel restricted to using your grill's side burners. There's really no reason you can't stick a big pot or pan right on your grill and use the burner heat the same you would on an inside stove. In fact, I hope by now you're starting to see your grill not just as a place to sizzle hamburgers and hotdogs, but also as your outdoor stove and oven. I truly love being in the kitchen, and I love being outdoors, so when I grill, I get the best of both worlds: an outdoor kitchen!

Make sure, however, that if you do use a pot or a pan that it's safe for very high heat. Not all pans are, especially some of the ones with nonstick or Teflon coating. You don't want that coating to melt off! (The same goes for plastic handles.) If your cookware is rated for oven use, you're OK. Or get stuff specifically made for camping. Just one roasting pan and one Dutch oven would be great, and you can even store them outside with your grill if it has any of those extra doors or drawers.

In my family, we're not big on going back into the kitchen to scrub dirty pots and pans after we've eaten, so we use a lot of disposable aluminum pans. You can't sauté or sear a steak in them or anything, but for cooking juicy seafood and pasta and letting their flavors mingle, they're perfect.

LEFTOVER PASTA

I hate to throw away extra food. I just can't bring myself to do it. It feels like a sin. But more often than not, we have extra pasta left over. It's not so great reheated the next day (although I do like it tossed in a pan with a little olive oil and some fresh herbs), and I don't care what your grandmother says, there's no point in freezing it.

So what can you do with leftover pasta? You can add extra sauce, put it in an oven-safe pan, top it with some cheese, and bake up a spaghetti pie. Or you can turn it into an amazing frittata.

Frittata is from the Italian word for "fry," and while it uses eggs and cheese like a quiche, it's fluffier and usually also contains pasta. Put a little olive oil on the bottom of an oven-safe pan, and add your leftover pasta. Depending on how much pasta you have, beat four to six eggs really well to get a lot of air into them. (A whisk is best for this job, but a fork is fine, too.) Add some salt and pepper, then pour the eggs over the pasta. Sprinkle your favorite cheese over the top—mozzarella, Pecorino Romano, fontina—and then bake at 300°F for thirty minutes, until the egg is set and the cheese is starting to brown. Let it set for another five minutes before serving. No need to even tell your guests they're eating leftovers—they'll never notice!

Grilled Vegetable Lasagna

Makes 9 to 12 servings

I'm not gonna lie—this is a bit of a project, but you won't care when you hear all your guests raving, "This is the most outrageously delicious lasagna I've ever eaten!" And no-boil noodles cut the hassle factor down a lot. If you have any vegetarians in the family, this is one time when the tables will be turned on the carnivores, who won't even notice that there isn't any meat.

2 large eggplants, cut into
½-inch-thick rounds

Extra-virgin olive oil, for
brushing the vegetables and
the baking dish

½ teaspoon salt, plus more
for seasoning

½ teaspoons freshly ground black
pepperplus more for seasoning

2 medium zucchini, cut lengthwise
into ½-inch-thick strips

2 red bell peppers, cut according
to the instructions on page 180

4 cups (1 pound) shredded
mozzarella cheese, divided

1 (15-ounce) container
ricotta cheese

1 cup (4 ounces) freshly grated
Parmesan cheese

¼ cup finely chopped fresh basil

1 recipe "The Quickie" Tomato
Sauce with Garlic (page 56)

12 no-boil lasagna noodles

1. Preheat the grill for direct cooking over medium heat (400°F).

2. Brush the eggplant rounds on both sides with the oil and season with the salt and pepper. Place the eggplant rounds directly on the grill and close the lid. Cook until the undersides are seared with grill marks, about 5 minutes. Flip the eggplant rounds and continue cooking, with the lid closed, until the other sides are seared and the eggplant is tender when pierced with the tip of a small knife, about 5 minutes more. Transfer to a platter.

3. Repeat with the zucchini slices, cooking until just tender, with the lid closed as much as possible, about 5 minutes total. Transfer to the platter with the eggplant.

4. Increase the grill temperature to high (500°F). Place the peppers on the grill and cook according to the instructions on page 178. Coarsely chop the peppers and add to the platter.

5. Put 3 cups of the mozzarella in a medium bowl, reserving the remaining mozzarella for the topping. Add the ricotta, Parmesan, and basil to the bowl and mix well. Season lightly with salt and pepper.

6. Lightly oil a 13 x 9-inch baking dish that is at least 2 inches deep. Spread ¾ cup of the tomato sauce in the bottom of the dish. Top with 4 overlapping lasagna noodles, one-third of the remaining tomato sauce, and half of the cheese mixture, spread as evenly as possible. Arrange half of the vegetables as evenly as possible over the cheese mixture. Repeat with 4 more noodles, the remaining cheese mixture, half of the remaining tomato sauce, and the remaining vegetables. Finish with the remaining noodles, spread with the remaining tomato sauce, and sprinkle the reserved mozzarella on top. Cover loosely with an oiled piece of aluminum foil, oiled side down, tenting the foil so it does not touch the cheese. (The lasagna can be refrigerated for 2 hours before cooking.)

7. Preheat the grill for indirect cooking with medium-low heat (350°).

8. Place the baking dish on the grill over the unignited burner(s) and close the grill lid. Cook for 45 minutes. Remove the foil and continue cooking until the sauce is bubbling and the mozzarella topping is golden brown, about 30 minutes more. Remove the baking dish from the grill. Let stand for 15 minutes. Cut into serving portions and serve hot.

Note: You can bake the lasagna in a preheated 350°F oven, if you prefer.

Ziti with Grilled Meatballs and Tomato Sauce

Makes 4 to 6 servings

Grilling meatballs not only adds extra flavor to them, but it also keeps your stove clean from annoying grease splatters. You'll want to cook the meatballs on a perforated grill pan, or use a perforated meatball holder specifically made for grilling. If you use the holder, just shape the meatball mixture, put the balls in the oiled holder, and grill for about six minutes per side.

Meatballs:

1 pound ground round beef

½ cup Italian-seasoned dry bread crumbs

½ cup milk (preferably 2%)

⅓ cup plus 1 tablespoon freshly grated Pecorino Romano cheese

1 large egg, beaten

3 tablespoons finely chopped fresh flat-leaf parsley

2 garlic cloves, minced

¾ teaspoon salt

¼ teaspoon freshly ground black pepper

Extra-virgin olive oil, for brushing and for the pan

1 recipe "The Quickie" Tomato Sauce with Garlic (page 56)

½ teaspoon red pepper flakes

1 pound ziti or other tube-shaped pasta

Freshly grated Parmesan cheese, for serving

1. To make the meatballs: Combine the ground round, bread crumbs, milk, grated Pecorino Romano cheese, egg, parsley, garlic, salt, and pepper in a large bowl. Mix everything together with clean hands. Feel for the right texture—it should be soft, but not sopping wet, so add a little more milk (if it's too dry) or bread crumbs (if it's too wet), if needed. Shape into 12 equal balls by gently shaping the meat mixture in your hands. Do not crush and mold the meat between your palms. Place the balls on a plate and brush all over with oil. Refrigerate the meatballs while preheating the grill.

2. Preheat the grill for direct cooking over medium heat (400°F).

3. Lightly oil a perforated grill pan, place it on the cooking grate, close the grill lid, and heat for 2 minutes. Place the meatballs on the pan. Cook, with the lid closed as much as possible, turning the meatballs occasionally with a metal spatula, until browned on all sides, about 12 minutes. The meatballs do not have to be cooked through. Remove the pan from the grill.

4. Meanwhile, bring a large pot of salted water to a boil over high heat.

5. Bring the tomato sauce and red pepper flakes to a simmer in a large saucepan over medium heat. Add the grilled meatballs and reduce the heat to medium-low. Simmer until the meatballs show no sign of pink when pierced in the center, about 15 minutes.

6. Add the ziti to the water and cook according to the package directions until al dente. Drain well. Return the pasta to the pot. Add the sauce and meatballs and mix well.

7. Transfer to a serving bowl. Serve hot with the Parmesan cheese passed on the side.

✴ ✴ ✴ The Pasta Monster ✴ ✴ ✴

An idea of how much we love our pasta in Italy? Instead of saying you caught someone with their hand "in the cookie jar," we say *beccare con le mani in pasta,* which means caught with your hand in the pasta.

Penne with Grilled Portobellos and Creamy Pesto

Makes 4 to 6 servings

Italians don't cook with heavy cream a lot . . . unlike the French, who put it in everything. So, when I use it, you know the dish is really special. That's how I feel about this pasta, which has meaty grilled mushrooms, zesty pesto, and sinfully rich cream. And it's a perfect example of how a jar of (homemade) pesto in your fridge can make a meal magical.

6 (4-inch) portobello
    mushroom caps
Extra-virgin olive oil, for brushing
    the mushrooms
Salt and freshly ground
    black pepper
1 pound penne or other tube-
    shaped pasta
½ cup Homemade Pesto
    (facing page)
½ cup freshly grated Parmesan
    cheese, plus more for serving
⅓ cup heavy cream

1. Preheat the grill for direct cooking over medium heat (400°F).

2. Brush the mushrooms on both sides with oil and season with salt and pepper. Place on the cooking grate, gill-sides up, and close the grill lid. Cook until the undersides are seared with grill marks, about 3 minutes. Flip the mushrooms and continue cooking, with the lid closed, until tender, 3 to 4 minutes more. Transfer to a plate and tent with aluminum foil to keep warm.

3. Meanwhile, bring a large pot of salted water to a boil over high heat. Add the penne and cook according to the package directions until al dente. Scoop out and reserve ½ cup of the cooking water and then drain the pasta well. Return the pasta to the pot.

4. Cut the mushrooms into bite-size pieces. Add to the pot of pasta, along with the pesto, Parmesan cheese, and cream. Stir, adding enough of the pasta water to make a light sauce. Season with salt and pepper. Serve hot, with additional Parmesan cheese passed on the side.

Homemade Pesto

Makes about 1 cup

Pesto is a magical ingredient, and during the summer, when basil is cheap at our local farmer and markets, I made big batches to put in everything. (OK, maybe not on dessert . . .) If you want to freeze it, don't put the cheese in or top with oil before freezing. When ready to serve, thaw for a few hours at room temperature (don't use the microwave or the pesto will turn dark), and then add as much cheese as you like.

⅓ cup pine nuts

3 garlic cloves, crushed

1½ cups packed fresh basil leaves

½ cup freshly grated Parmigiano-
    Reggiano cheese

⅔ cup extra virgin olive oil, plus
    more if storing for later use

¼ teaspoon salt

⅛ teaspoon freshly ground black
    pepper

1. Heat a small skillet over medium heat. Add the pine nuts and cook, stirring occasionally, until lightly toasted, about 2 minutes. Transfer to a plate and let cool completely.

2. Fit a food processor with a metal chopping blade. With the machine running, drop the garlic through the feed tube to mince it. Add the toasted pine nuts and pulse until finely chopped. Add the basil leaves and pulse until finely chopped. Add the cheese and pulse to combine. With the machine running, gradually pour in the oil. (You can also do this in batches in a blender, stopping the blender occasionally to stir down the ingredients.) Add the salt and pepper.

3. Transfer the pesto to an airtight container. Pour in enough oil to cover the pesto with a thin film. (This seals the pesto and helps keep it from molding.) Refrigerate for up to 6 weeks. (Or, omit the cheese and final oil topping, and freeze for up to 6 months. Thaw at room temperature before using.)

Spaghetti with Grilled Tuna Puttanesca

Makes 4 to 6 servings

Pardon my French, but *puttana* is the Italian word for "whore." Puttanesca then is anything that is made in the "whore's style," which means thrown together quickly and cheaply. (Ain't that the truth?) Puttanesca traditionally uses (stinky) canned tuna, but we're going to class it up a bit (meaning, this recipe isn't as quick or cheap!) and use delicious grilled tuna steaks and fresh (instead of the usual canned) tomatoes. See, the good girl's way is *always* better!

Sauce:

3 pounds plum (Roma) tomatoes, cut in half lengthwise

¼ cup extra-virgin olive oil, plus more for brushing the tomatoes

Salt and freshly ground black pepper

3 garlic cloves, minced

½ cup packed basil leaves

¼ teaspoon red pepper flakes

½ cup pitted and coarsely chopped Kalamata olives

3 tablespoons drained and rinsed capers, chopped if large

2 tablespoons drained chopped anchovy fillets

Tuna:

2 tuna steaks (each 6 ounces and cut 1 inch thick)

Extra-virgin olive oil, for brushing

½ teaspoon salt

¼ teaspoon freshly ground black pepper

1 pound spaghetti

1. Preheat the grill for indirect cooking with medium heat (400°F).

2. To make the sauce: Arrange the tomatoes, cut sides up, in a metal roasting pan. Brush lightly with oil and season with salt and pepper. Place the pan over the unignited burner(s) and close the lid. Cook until the tomatoes are very tender and their edges are browned, about 1 hour. Remove the pan from the grill.

3. Preheat the grill for direct cooking over high heat (500°F).

4. To make the tuna: Lightly brush the tuna on both sides with oil and season with the salt and pepper. Place the tuna on the cooking grate and close the grill. Cook until the undersides are seared with grill marks, about 2½ minutes. Flip the tuna and continue cooking, with the lid closed, until the other sides are seared and the tuna is opaque on the outside with a rosy pink center when cut with a small sharp knife, about 2½ minutes more. Transfer the tuna to a plate.

5. Meanwhile, bring a large pot of salted water to a boil over high heat. Add the spaghetti and cook according to the package directions until al dente.

6. While the pasta is cooking, finish the sauce: Heat ¼ cup of the oil and the garlic in a large saucepan over medium heat until the garlic is tender, but not browned, about 2 minutes. Pour the garlic oil into a food processor and add the tomatoes, basil, and red pepper flakes. Process the tomato mixture until coarsely chopped. Return the tomato sauce to the saucepan. (If you don't have a food processor, add the tomatoes to the garlic oil in the saucepan and break up the tomatoes with a potato masher to make a chunky sauce. Chop the basil and stir it into the sauce, with the red pepper flakes.)

7. Add the olives, capers, and anchovies to the tomato sauce and bring just to a simmer over medium heat, stirring often. Cut the tuna into bite-size pieces. Add to the tomato sauce, stir well, and remove from the heat.

8. Drain the pasta well. Return to its cooking pot. Add the sauce and stir to combine. Serve hot.

Fusilli with Grilled Sausages, Zucchini, and Ricotta

Makes 4 to 6 servings

In a perfect world, you would time the sausage and zucchini to come off the grill when the pasta is just finished cooking. Don't worry if they cool off a bit though, because they will heat up again when mixed with the hot pasta. Leave out the sausage, if you wish, for a vegetarian version.

6 links sweet Italian sausage (about 1¼ pounds), each pierced with a fork

3 large zucchini, cut lengthwise into ½-inch-thick slices

Extra-virgin olive oil, for brushing the zucchini

Salt and freshly ground black pepper

1 pound fusilli

1 cup halved cherry or grape tomatoes

½ cup freshly grated Pecorino Romano cheese, plus more for serving

1 tablespoon finely chopped fresh oregano

Red pepper flakes

3/4 cup ricotta cheese

1. Preheat the grill for direct cooking over medium-high heat (450°F).

2. Place the sausages directly on the grate and close the grill lid. Cook, turning occasionally, until the sausages are cooked through, about 12 minutes. Transfer the sausages to a platter and tent with aluminum foil.

3. Brush the zucchini on both sides with oil and season with salt and pepper. Place on the grate, perpendicular to the grid, and close the lid. Cook until the undersides are seared with grill marks, about 2½ minutes. Flip the zucchini and continue cooking, with the lid closed, until they are crisp-tender, about 2½ minutes more. Add the zucchini to the platter and tent with foil.

4. Meanwhile, bring a large pot of salted water to a boil over high heat. Add the fusilli and cook according to the package directions until al dente. Scoop out and reserve ½ cup of the pasta cooking water. Drain the pasta and return it to the pot.

5. Cut the sausages and zucchini into bite-size pieces. Add them to the pasta, along with the tomatoes, Romano, and oregano. Stir, adding enough of the pasta cooking water to make a light sauce. Season with salt and red pepper flakes. Transfer to a serving bowl and top with the ricotta. Toss and serve hot, with additional Romano cheese passed on the side.

Jersey Shore Seafood Pasta

Makes 6 to 8 servings

This is another classic aluminum-pan-on-the-grill recipe. My dad is the expert in making this dish, and he loves to throw the cooked linguini directly into the pan on the grill, right on top of the seafood, so the pasta gets all "juiced" up. Try to time the pasta so it's done about the same time as the seafood. If things don't seem to be cooking at the same rate, just use tongs to transfer the cooked items to a bowl and cover with foil to keep warm.

This makes serving to company a bit of a challenge though, so I'm giving you directions on how to keep it all pretty for plating. There are a few options for the seafood, so enjoy your favorites. Just be sure to allow time to soak the clams or mussels.

1½ pounds linguine

¼ cup plus 2 tablespoons extra-virgin olive oil

4 tablespoons (½ stick) unsalted butter

12 garlic cloves, minced

1 cup dry white wine, such as Pinot Grigio

1 cup bottled clam juice

3 tablespoons finely chopped fresh flat-leaf parsley

½ teaspoon red pepper flakes

3 dozen littleneck clams or mussels (or a combination), scrubbed under cold water, soaked in cold salted ice water for at least 1 and up to 2 hours, and drained

6 blue crabs, cleaned by the fish store

1 pound extra-large (26 to 30 count) shrimp, peeled and deveined, or large sea scallops

✳ ✳ ✳ Cleaning Blue Crabs ✳ ✳ ✳

Blue crabs, named for the color of their claws, are the small crustaceans (about the width of a saucer) that we have on the Jersey Shore. To clean them, you need to remove the top shell, discard the gills, and rinse out the crab to remove the innards . . . while the crab is still alive. Um, no thank you! I'm lucky that I have a husband and a father that love to clean crabs, but if you don't, don't worry! Most places that sell blue crabs will clean them for you, especially if you give the worker a tip. Or you can just skip the blue crab entirely (although it is sweet and delicious!) and increase the shrimp and other seafood.

1. Bring a large pot of salted water to a boil over high heat.

2. While the water is heating, preheat the grill for direct cooking over medium heat (400°F).

3. Place a large, disposable, aluminum foil roasting pan on the cooking grate. Add ¼ cup of oil, butter, and garlic and close the grill lid. Cook, stirring often, until the butter is melted and the garlic is fragrant and softened, about 3 minutes. Stir in the wine, clam juice, parsley, and red pepper flakes. Put the clams and crabs in the bottom of the pan. Close the grill lid. Cook for 5 minutes. Shake the pan well, and scatter the shrimp on top of the clams and crabs. Continue cooking, with the lid closed, occasionally shaking the pan, until the clams have opened and the shrimp is opaque, 5 to 10 minutes more.

4. About 10 minutes before the seafood is done, add the linguine to the pot of boiling water and cook according to the package directions until al dente. Drain well. Transfer to a large serving bowl, toss with the remaining 2 tablespoons oil, and cover with aluminum foil to keep warm.

5. Remove the roasting pan from the grill. Using tongs and a slotted spoon, transfer the seafood to a large bowl, discarding any unopened clams.

6. Pour the cooking liquid in the pan over the pasta and mix well. Divide the pasta and sauce among deep soup bowls, and top with equal amounts of the seafood. Serve hot.

Summer Spaghetti with Grilled Tomato and Basil Sauce

Makes 4 to 6 servings

This grilled sauce is fantastic with spaghetti, but you can also use it for any other pasta and with any other additions: add grilled shrimp or sausage—or both! Fair warning though, the reason I call this "summer spaghetti" is because it's only worth making with ripe local tomatoes.

Sauce:

3 pounds ripe plum (Roma) tomatoes, cut in half lengthwise

¼ cup plus 2 tablespoons extra-virgin olive oil

Salt and freshly ground black pepper

3 garlic cloves, minced

½ cup packed basil leaves

¼ teaspoon red pepper flakes

1 pound spaghetti

Freshly grated Parmesan cheese, for serving

1. Preheat the grill for indirect cooking with medium heat (400°F).

2. Arrange the tomatoes, cut sides up, in a metal roasting pan. Brush with 2 tablespoons of oil and season with salt and pepper. Place the pan over the unignited burner(s) and close the lid. Cook until the tomatoes are very tender and their edges are browned, about 1 hour. Remove the pan from the grill.

3. Heat the remaining ¼ cup oil and the garlic over medium heat until the garlic is tender, about 2 minutes. Remove from the heat. Pulse the tomatoes, garlic oil, basil, and red pepper flakes in a food processor until coarsely chopped. (If you don't have a food processor, add the tomatoes to the garlic oil in the saucepan and mash with a potato masher into a chunky sauce. Chop the basil and stir it into the sauce, with the red pepper flakes.)

4. Meanwhile, bring a large pot of salted water to a boil over high heat. Add the spaghetti and cook according to the package directions until al dente. Drain well. Return the spaghetti to the pot and add the sauce. Stir to combine well.

5. Serve hot with the Parmesan cheese passed on the side.

CHAPTER 9

Contorni (Side Dishes)

Presto matura, presto marcio.

Literally: "Early ripe, early rotten."

What it means: If you spoil a young child too much

they will turn into a rotten adult.

I'm giving you some side dishes that feature my favorite summer vegetables: carrots, eggplant, peppers, and zucchini; but know that some of these recipes, like the grilled eggplant, can easily be made as entrées for vegetarians—or anyone really. I grew up eating lots of vegetables because my mother grew up the same way, and we were surrounded by them; in Italy there are 25 million acres of farmland that grow fruits and veggies.

If you've ever grown any summer vegetables yourself, you know it can be almost too easy, and you can easily end up with more than you'll ever eat. At the end of every summer in August, my family gets together and we can tomatoes to last us through the year, but we also preserve extra zucchini. Just like tomatoes, zucchini can be sun-dried, too.

In addition to preserving, my mother actually uses the sun to "prebake" vegetables too. For instance, she'll put the salted zucchini slices for *scapece* on a baking sheet and set them in the sun for an hour to let the salt pull out some of the moisture and concentrate the zucchini's taste. Try her "old world" trick and see if it doesn't make the Italian squash a little more special—just like my mama!

A New Season(ing): Paprika

Although it's not well known as an Italian seasoning, paprika is commonly used in many Italian dishes because it is, after all, just another form of one of our favorite ingredients: peppers. Red hot pepper flakes are an Italian staple, and paprika is made from ground, dried peppers. I use paprika a lot in my summer dishes because it's milder than cayenne pepper and has an almost fruity taste. It also makes any dish prettier!

Paprika belongs on more than just devilled eggs. I use it on chicken, salads, and once you taste it on my grilled corn on the cob, you won't want it any other way!

Grilled Eggplant with Pesto and Mozzarella

Makes 6 servings

Eggplant loves being grilled—it picks up a lot of flavor. Eggplant also loves garlic, olive oil, pesto, and Parmesan cheese, and when you put these all together, you end up with a kind of vegetable pizza without the dough. You can serve this as a side dish to just about any meat, or try it as a warm appetizer, maybe drizzled with a little balsamic vinegar. You can easily take this dish to a whole new level by serving it with my Quickie Tomato Sauce (page 56). It will magically transform into a new main course: Grilled Eggplant Parmesan.

⅓ cup extra-virgin olive oil

2 garlic cloves, crushed under the flat side of a knife and peeled

1 large eggplant, cut crosswise into ½-inch-thick rounds

1 teaspoon salt

½ teaspoon freshly ground black pepper

¼ cup Homemade Pesto (page 161)

⅓ cup freshly grated Parmesan cheese

1. Heat the oil and garlic together over medium-low heat until tiny bubbles form around the garlic, about 3 minutes. Remove the pan from the heat and set aside for at least 30 minutes and up to 1 hour. Discard the garlic.

2. Preheat the grill for direct cooking over medium heat (400°F).

3. Brush the eggplant rounds on one side with about half of the garlic oil. Season the eggplant on both sides with salt and pepper. Transfer to a large platter. Place the eggplant, oiled-sides down, on the cooking grate and cover with the grill lid. Cook until the underside is golden brown and seared with grill marks, about 5 minutes. Brush with the remaining garlic oil. Flip the eggplant over and continue to cook, with the lid closed, until the other side is golden brown and the eggplant is tender, about 5 minutes more. Flip the eggplant, and use the back of a spoon to spread each eggplant round with a thin smear of pesto. Sprinkle with the Parmesan cheese and cook with the lid closed until the cheese melts, about 1 minute.

4. Return the eggplant rounds to the platter, slightly overlapping. Serve hot or cooled to room temperature.

Contorni (Side Dishes)

Fabellini Glazed Carrots

Makes 6 servings

This is my Teresa twist on the French dish Carrots Vichy, in which root veggies are glazed with mineral water, butter, and sugar. In this recipe, though, I use my Fabellini fruit-flavored sparkling wine. It's a bit of a splurge for a side dish (unless you use the leftovers from the previous night's celebration), but the carrots turn out like candy, and everyone will *love* them.

1 tablespoon extra-virgin olive oil

1 tablespoon unsalted butter

1 pound baby-cut carrots

2 tablespoons light brown sugar

1½ cups raspberry-flavored sparkling wine, such as Fabellini

Salt and freshly ground black pepper

1 tablespoon finely chopped fresh flat-leaf parsley, for serving

1. Use a large nonstick skillet big enough to hold the baby carrots in a single layer. Heat the oil and butter together in the skillet over medium heat until the butter melts. Add the carrots and sprinkle with the brown sugar. Cook, stirring often, until the sugar is melted, about 2 minutes. Add the Fabellini, spread the carrots in a single layer, and bring to a simmer.

2. Reduce the heat to medium-low and cover the skillet. Simmer for 10 minutes, occasionally stirring the carrots. Uncover and increase the heat to high. Cook, stirring often, until the carrots are very tender and the liquid is syrupy and reduced to about 2 tablespoons, 10 to 15 minutes. Season with salt and pepper. Sprinkle with the parsley and serve hot.

Parmesan and Paprika Corn on the Cob

Makes 6 servings

Sweet summer corn on the cob grilled with butter is delicious. But you'll never want it that way again after you try it Italian-style, with garlic, smoked paprika, and Parmesan cheese.

8 tablespoons (1 stick) unsalted
  butter, at room temperature
1 teaspoon smoked sweet paprika
  (also called *pimentón de la Vera*)
1 garlic clove, crushed through
  a press
6 ears of corn, husked
1 cup freshly grated Parmesan
  cheese, as needed
Salt

1. Preheat the grill for direct cooking over medium heat (400°F). Brush the cooking grates clean.

2. Tear six 12-inch squares of heavy-duty aluminum foil. Mix the butter, paprika, and garlic together in a small bowl. Spread each corn ear with an equal amount of the garlic butter, place on the foil and roll it up tightly. (The corn can be stored at room temperature for up to 8 hours.)

3. Place the foil-wrapped corn on the cooking grate and cover with the grill lid. Cook, turning occasionally, until the corn is heated through with some toasted browned spots (open the foil to check), 12 to 15 minutes. Transfer the foil-wrapped corn to a platter.

4. Unwrap the corn and return to the platter. Serve hot, allowing each person to sprinkle the corn with Parmesan cheese and salt to taste before eating.

✳ ✳ ✳ **Paprika Primer** ✳ ✳ ✳

There are a few different varieties of paprika available, and you should pick the one that suits your palate. If you find paprika in a regular supermarket (look in the spice aisle) and it's not labeled as anything but "paprika," it's a mild version. The imported Hungarian or Spanish kinds have the most flavor. Hot paprika is labeled just that: "hot." There's also a Spanish smoked paprika (also called *pimentón de la Vera*) that I love.

✳ ✳ ✳ Grilling Peppers ✳ ✳ ✳

Grilled bell peppers are everywhere in Italian cooking, but I make them most in the summertime when they are in season. Red and yellow bell peppers really should be peeled, and charring over a flame helps loosen their thick skins for removal. (Green peppers have thinner skins and flesh, and don't need to be peeled.) Yes, you can cook them on the stove over an open gas flame or under a broiler, but grilling is the easiest way.

You probably know the method of putting the whole pepper on the grill and turning it until it is blackened, but there is an easier way that skips the turning. The trick is to cut the pepper open into a long strip so it lays flat on the grill.

Cut off the top and bottom from a bell pepper to make "lids." Discard the stem. Make a vertical cut down the side of the pepper and open up the pepper. Remove the core and seeds.

Preheat the grill for direct cooking over high heat (500°F). Place the pepper, skin-side down, directly on the cooking grate and close the grill lid. Cook, without turning, until the skins are blackened and blistered, taking care that you don't burn through the flesh, about 10 minutes. Transfer to a large bowl, cover with plastic wrap or a plate, and let stand for until tepid, about 20 minutes.

Using a small sharp knife as an aide, peel and scrape the blackened skin from the peppers. Don't rinse them under cold running water unless absolutely necessary to get rid of black flecks of skin. Cut the peppers on a chopping board into one-half-inch-wide strips and transfer to a medium bowl.

Grilled Peperonata

Makes about 2 cups, 6 servings

This peperonata has peppers that are grilled and marinated with capers, garlic, and oregano in a sweet-and-sour dressing. We serve it by itself, as a side, but you can also use it as a sauce on top of grilled pork chops, as an amazing bruschetta topping, or as a condiment on a salami sandwich on crusty bread.

2 medium red bell peppers

2 medium yellow bell peppers

1 tablespoon red wine vinegar

1 teaspoon dried oregano

1 teaspoon sugar

1/4 teaspoon red pepper flakes

2 garlic cloves, finely chopped

2 tablespoons extra-virgin olive oil

3 tablespoons bottled capers, rinsed and drained

Salt

1. Preheat the grill for direct cooking over high heat (500°F). Prepare and grill the peppers according to the instructions on facing page. Cool, peel, and cut into 1/2-inch-wide strips. Transfer to a medium bowl.

2. Whisk the vinegar, oregano, sugar, red pepper flakes, and garlic together in a small bowl. Whisk in the oil. Pour over the peppers, add the capers, and toss to coat. Season with salt to taste. Cover and refrigerate for at least 2 hours to allow the flavors to blend. (The peperonata can be refrigerated for up to 1 week.) Serve chilled or at room temperature.

Alici Baked Potatoes

Makes 6 servings

Anchovies and potatoes are a great combination, and whenever I serve these, people usually don't know that it has anchovies until I tell them. It's easiest to bake the potatoes inside (or use the microwave), and then put the stuffed halves on the grill to heat up before serving. You can put the potatoes over the empty side of the grill to cook with indirect heat, and cook meat over the ignited burner at the same time. These are fantastic with steaks or pork chops.

3 large baking potatoes, scrubbed but unpeeled
2 tablespoons unsalted butter
3 tablespoons whole milk
4 anchovy fillets in oil, drained and finely chopped
Salt and red pepper flakes
Extra-virgin olive oil, for drizzling
Finely chopped fresh flat-leaf parsley, for serving

1. Preheat the oven to 350°F. Pierce each potato a few times with a fork. Bake directly on the oven rack until tender when pierced with the tip of a sharp knife, about 45 minutes. Let cool until easy to handle, about 15 minutes.

2. Cut each potato in half lengthwise. Using a spoon, scoop out the potato flesh from each potato half into a medium bowl, leaving a shell about 1/2 inch thick. Add the butter to the bowl, and using a fork, mash the potatoes, gradually stirring in the milk. Stir in the anchovies. Season with salt and red pepper flakes to taste. Spoon the mixture into the potato shells. (The potatoes can be covered with plastic wrap and kept at room temperature for up to 1 hour.)

3. Preheat the grill for indirect cooking with high heat (500°F).

4. Drizzle oil over the stuffed potatoes. Place on the cooking grate and cover with the grill lid. Cook until heated through, about 10 minutes. Remove from the grill, sprinkle with the parsley, and serve hot.

Grilled Zucchini Scapece

Makes 6 servings

When you see that a food (usually vegetables or fish) is prepared *scapece*-style, it means that it has been marinated in a tart vinegar sauce. My mama always salts the zucchini first, to draw out its excess juice so that the juices don't dilute the marinade. This is another dish that you are likely to see on an antipasti menu, but it can double as a side dish. Try it with simple grilled fish steaks or fillets (see photo on page 176).

3 large zucchini, cut lengthwise into ¼- to ½-inch-thick strips
1 teaspoon salt
¼ cup extra-virgin olive oil, plus more for brushing the zucchini
Freshly ground black pepper
2 tablespoons white wine vinegar
2 tablespoons balsamic vinegar
1 garlic clove, minced

1. Arrange the zucchini strips on a baking sheet and sprinkle on both sides with 1 teaspoon of salt. Let stand for 30 minutes to 1 hour. Rinse under cold running water and pat dry on clean kitchen towels or paper towels.

2. Preheat the grill for direct cooking over medium heat (400°F).

3. Return the zucchini to the baking sheet and brush lightly on both sides with oil. Season with pepper. Place the zucchini on the cooking grates, perpendicular to the grid, and cover with the grill lid. Cook until the zucchini undersides are seared with grill marks, about 3 minutes. Flip the zucchini and continue cooking until seared and crisp-tender, about 2 minutes more. Remove the zucchini from the grill.

4. Arrange the zucchini in a deep serving platter. Whisk the white wine and balsamic vinegar with the garlic in a small bowl. Gradually whisk in ½ cup of oil. Pour evenly over the zucchini, and turn the zucchini to coat with the vinegar mixture. Let stand for at least 1 hour. (Or cover and refrigerate for up to 2 days. Let stand at room temperature for 1 hour before serving.) Serve at room temperature.

CHAPTER 10

Dolci (Desserts)

Quando la pera è matura, casca da sè.

Literally: "When the pear is matured, it will fall by itself."

What it means: "All things happen in their own good time."

In rural Italy, a true, traditional dessert menu following a summer meal would read like this: fruit, fruit, or fruit. Wine. Wine with fruit. More wine. Fruit.

The only time people eat baked goods, cookies, or cannoli are at carnivals, saints' days, holidays, and celebrations like weddings and christenings. The rest of the time, dessert is simple and naturally sweet: fruit.

Of course, restaurants—mainly the ones catering to American tourists—serve our special national treats every day, so we're going to do the same thing here. All of my own sweet summer recipes—except one—do include fruit. The exception is a chocolate hazelnut gelato-like semifreddo (page 195), and I think we can all make an exception for that!

PEACHES, ITALIAN-STYLE

If you've ever been to Hawaii and tasted the pineapple there, you know that the stuff we get on the mainland doesn't come even close to tasting as good. The same is true of peaches in the Mediterranean. They are so delicious that it's hard to even describe.

Peaches are obviously a very fragile fruit, but they also stop producing sugar once they're picked, so if they're picked too early (and the farther they have to travel from tree to store, the earlier they will get picked), they are never going to be as sweet as they could be. The closer you live to where the fruit is actually grown, the better it's going to be. That's why I get fresh produce from farmers' markets and roadside farm stands every chance I get.

Unless you live on an orchard, though, you're going to have to get fruit from the store sometimes. Here's how to find the best summer fruit.

Picking Fantastic Fresh Fruit

Apples: This is one fruit where the brightest and shiniest color doesn't really mean it tastes the best. (In fact, that "shine" is usually sprayed on commercially grown apples.) The most important thing is to get a firm, unblemished apple. And this is the one fruit I would always buy organic if you can because of the amount of pesticides you'll save your body from. Organic apples aren't as shiny on the outside, but they're just as delicious and juicy on the inside. Apples will last the longest when stored in the fridge.

Blueberries: Look for berries that are blue—not red or purple—and have a slightly waxy shine to them (that's natural). You want blueberries that are plump, firm, and all the same size. Like other berries, make sure they are dry; pass on packages with leaks or stains. Store in the fridge, and don't wash until just before eating them.

Oranges: Water is heavier than pulp so if you want a juicy orange, pick one that's heavy for its size. Also look for bright-colored skin with no blemishes.

Peaches: First, a peach should smell like a peach. If you don't get a rich, ripe, fruity smell off of it, it's never going to taste very good. Look for a deep cleft and firm skin that gives just a little when you press on it. Store peaches at room temperature, with plenty of air around each one, and use them within a few days.

Raspberries and Blackberries: Avoid dull-colored berries: raspberries should be medium to bright red; blackberries should be shiny and black. Look for dry berries; any moisture or juice is a sign of decay or decay to come. Store in the fridge uncovered, and don't wash until just before you use them.

Strawberries: When it comes to taste, bright red and shiny matters more than size. Look for ones with even color, a healthy green cap that's still attached, and a nice fresh aroma. Don't get any with brown or white spots as decay can spread to nearby strawberries in a matter of hours. If you can, buy strawberries the same day you plan to use them. Store them unwashed and uncut in the crisper drawer of your fridge. Don't wash until right before you're ready to serve them.

Watermelon: You want a melon with brightly colored green skin, although it should have a yellow spot on the bottom where it sat on the ground when it was naturally ripening in the sun. Look for a melon that's symmetrical, doesn't have any dings or cuts, feels heavy, and sounds hollow when you thump it.

✳ ✳ ✳ Dreamy Desserts ✳ ✳ ✳

When I was choosing recipes for this book, I thought about making sure every single one could be made on the grill, but when it came to desserts, it just didn't make sense. Grilled peaches are divine because the heat caramelizes them, but most other sweets aren't so great on the grate. I could certainly invent some, but I'm all about authentic Italian cooking, and there just isn't anything remotely Mediterranean about a grilled banana or melty marshmallow anything. So instead I decided to give you my favorite warm weather treats including a quick cassata cake, refreshing drinks, and the best almost-ice cream you've ever eaten, a chocolate hazelnut semifreddo—all perfect ways to end your hot backyard meal.

Summer Cassata Cake

Makes 10 to 12 servings

A traditional cassata cake is a sponge cake soaked in fruit liqueur, stuffed with ricotta cheese, and topped with chocolate and candied fruit. Here's a quick summer version that uses store-bought angel food cake as a little (calorie-saving) treat, rum instead of liqueur (or you can use orange juice to make it nonalcoholic), and doesn't require any baking!

1 (15-ounce) container
    ricotta cheese
¼ cup plus 2 tablespoons
    confectioners' sugar
Grated zest of 1 orange, *optional*
3 tablespoons rum or fresh
    orange juice
½ cup miniature semisweet
    chocolate chips
1 store-bought angel food cake,
    about 7 inches in diameter
1½ cups heavy cream
½ teaspoon vanilla extract
1 block semisweet chocolate,
    at least 4 ounces
8 strawberries,
    cut in half vertically

1. Line a wire sieve with paper towels and place over a medium bowl. Spoon the ricotta into the sieve and let stand for 10 minutes to drain. Blot the top of the ricotta with additional paper towels.

2. Transfer the drained ricotta to another medium bowl, being careful to remove the paper towels. Using an electric mixer on high speed, beat the ricotta in a medium bowl until smooth. Beat in ¼ cup of the confectioners' sugar and the orange juice, followed by the chocolate chips.

3. Using a serrated knife, cut the cake crosswise into thirds. Place the bottom cake layer on a serving platter, and brush with 1 tablespoon of the rum. Spread with half of the ricotta mixture. Top with the middle layer, brush with another tablespoon of rum, and spread with the remaining ricotta mixture. Add the top cake layer and brush with the remaining rum.

4. Whip the cream, remaining 2 tablespoons confectioners' sugar, and vanilla together in a medium bowl with an electric mixer on high speed until very stiff peaks form. Spread the whipped cream mixture over the top and sides of the cake. Grate about half of the chocolate over the top of the cake. Refrigerate the cake, uncovered, for at least 1 hour or up to 12 hours before serving.

5. Just before serving, insert the strawberries, cut-sides up, into the cake, spacing them around the bottom of the cake. Serve chilled.

Italian Peach "Sangria"

Makes 6 servings

"Vintage" Italians, as I like to call my parents' generation, follow most meals like this: they slice fresh peaches, put them in a glass, pour red wine over the top, and then spend the rest of the evening spearing out the fruit with the tip of a knife. They eat, drink, eat, drink, repeat. I turned their tradition into an Italian "sangria" by mixing peaches with sugar in a pitcher (the sugar helps the peaches release some juice) and then adding the wine. While my parents like it room temperature, I prefer it chilled.

2 ripe peaches, pitted and cut into ½ inch slices
2 tablespoons sugar
1 (750-ml) bottle fruity red wine, such as merlot

1. Combine the peaches and sugar in a glass pitcher. Let stand at room temperature about 1 hour, or until the peaches give off some juices.

2. Pour in the red wine and stir well. Cover and refrigerate until chilled, at least 2 hours and up to 8 hours.

3. Pour into wine glasses, making sure that each glass gets some peaches. Serve chilled.

Una cena senza vino è come un giorno senza sole.
"A meal without wine is like a day without sunshine."

Joe's Juicy Applesauce

Makes about 1 quart

We always have homemade applesauce in our fridge. We eat it plain for breakfast and put it on roast chicken and turkey for dinner—but our favorite way to enjoy it is to spoon it over ice cream for dessert. The applesauce will change according to the kind of apples you use—McIntosh apples make a soft sauce, Golden Delicious apples make chunky sauce. Just taste the sauce before you serve it. It may be perfect for your palate, or you may want to sweeten it with a little sugar, or add some tartness with a splash of lemon juice.

....

3 pounds apples, such as Macoun, McIntosh, Golden Delicious, or Empire, peeled, cored, and cut into 1-inch chunks
Sugar, *optional*
Fresh lemon juice, *optional*

1. Put the apples in a large saucepan and add enough water to barely cover them. Bring to a boil over high heat.

2. Reduce the heat to medium and cook at a brisk simmer, stirring often, until the apples have broken down into a sauce, about 20 minutes. Reduce the heat to low and simmer, stirring often, until the applesauce is the desired thickness, 10 to 20 minutes longer, making sure that it doesn't scorch on the bottom. Taste the applesauce and adjust the flavor, if needed, with sugar or lemon juice. Serve warm or cool, cover, and refrigerate for up to 2 weeks.

Grilled Peach Sundaes with Caramel Sauce

Makes 6 servings

Grilling peaches brings their juices to the surface, where they take on a caramel flavor. Add a homemade caramel sauce, and it's summer-flavored heaven. Feel free to drizzle a little Amaretto or peach schnapps over the ice cream, too. But without the booze, this is a great, kid-friendly dessert. Just hold off until you get good, ripe, flavorful peaches, as the sauce and grilling won't really "fix" bad ones.

Caramel Sauce:
4 tablespoons unsalted butter
¾ cup packed light brown sugar
¾ cup heavy cream
1 teaspoon vanilla extract
Pinch of salt

Grilled Peaches:
6 ripe peaches, pitted
Vegetable oil, for brushing

1 quart peach, toasted almond, or vanilla ice cream, or a combination
Whipped cream, for serving (optional)
½ cup sliced natural almonds, toasted (see Teresa's Tip), for serving

1. To make the caramel sauce: Melt the butter in a medium, tall saucepan over medium heat. Add the brown sugar and stir until melted and bubbling. Cook, stirring often, for 2 minutes. Gradually stir in the cream—it will bubble up, so be very careful that it doesn't overflow the saucepan. Let cook, stirring often, until slightly thickened and reduced to about 1 cup, about 3 minutes. Remove from the heat. Stir in the vanilla and salt. Let cool completely. (The sauce can be stored at room temperature for up to 8 hours. It will thicken more as it stands.)

2. Preheat the grill for direct cooking over medium heat (400°F).

3. To grill the peaches: Lightly brush the peaches all over with the oil. Place on the cooking grate, cut-sides down, and cover with the grill lid. Cook until the undersides are seared with grill marks, about 3 minutes. Flip the peaches over and continue cooking, with the lid closed, until they are heated through and the juices are bubbling, about 3 minutes more. Remove from the grill. Let the peaches cool for a few minutes until they are warm, not piping, hot.

4. For each serving, place 2 peach halves in a bowl. Add a large scoop of ice cream and drizzle with about 2½ tablespoons of sauce. Top with a dollop of whipped cream, if using, and a sprinkle of toasted almonds. Serve immediately.

Teresa's Tip

A toaster oven is a great appliance for toasting almonds, pine nuts, walnuts, and other nuts because it won't heat up the house like a large oven does. Preheat the toaster oven to 350°F. Spread the almonds on the tray, and bake, mixing occasionally, until lightly browned and fragrant, about ten minutes. (You can also spread the almonds on a baking sheet and toast them in a conventional oven at 350°F for the same length of time.) Let cool completely.

Non si può avere la botte piena e la moglie ubriaca.
Literally: "You can't have a full barrel of wine and a drunk wife."
What it means: "You can't have your cake and eat it too."

Grownup Fabellini Sorbet

Makes 6 servings

The creaminess of sorbet really compliments a fizzy, fruity sparkling wine, and make an amazing dessert. You can mix and match the sorbet and fruit (there's no reason why you couldn't use strawberries or blueberries if you have them), and even substitute fruit soda for the wine to serve to the kids. But I love this "Melba" combination of raspberries and peach-flavored wine.

1½ pints raspberry sorbet

½ pint (6 ounces) fresh raspberries

1 (750-ml) bottle peach-flavored sparkling wine, such as Fabellini

Scoop the ice cream into six chilled wine glasses. Divide the raspberries among the glasses. Slowly fill each glass with the chilled wine. Serve immediately.

Watermelon Granita

Makes about 2 quarts

Granita is sorbet's country cousin. It's not very refined or smooth, but everyone loves it anyway. You don't need an ice cream maker for this fruity iced dessert, just a freezer. Watermelon is the dessert of choice at many backyard cookouts, and when it is made into granita, it's easier to eat, and you don't have to spit out the seeds.

6 pounds watermelon,
    preferably seedless
3/4 cup sugar
2 tablespoons fresh lemon juice

1. Place a metal 13 x 9-inch baking pan in the freezer and let chill while preparing the granita.

2. Cut the watermelon flesh into chunks, discarding the seeds and rind. In batches, purée the watermelon in a blender. You should have 6 cups purée. Process 1 cup of the purée with the sugar and lemon juice in the blender until the sugar dissolves. Stir back into the remaining purée.

3. Pour the mixture into the chilled pan. Freeze until the sides of the mixture are partially frozen and slushy, about 1½ hours. Using a fork, mix the frozen edges into the center (leave the fork in the pan). Freeze, repeating the stirring procedure about every 30 minutes, until the mixture has a slushy consistency, about 3 hours total freezing time. (The granita can be made up to one day ahead. If it freezes too hard, just scrape the mixture with fork tines to make it into slush.)

4. Spoon the granita into chilled glasses and serve immediately.

✴✴✴ Watermel-ON ✴✴✴

Like another watery red fruit—tomatoes—watermelon are chock full of the antioxidant lycopene. And because it contains an amino acid called citrulline, which helps relax blood vessels, watermelon is known as the "natural Viagra." More, please!

Baci Semifreddo

Makes 6 to 8 servings

As always, I had to leave you with a happy ending. This time, with *baci*—"kisses" in Italian. Gelato is amazing, but requires an ice cream machine to make. Semifreddo, which means "half-frozen," is a soft, spoon-able, homemade ice cream that can be made in a regular freezer. Add the fact that it's a chocolate-hazelnut flavor and uses my favorites—Nutella and Baci candies—and you'll agree with my friend who says this is the best thing she's had in her mouth since her honeymoon. You're welcome.

....

1 cup heavy cream, divided

½ cup Nutella or other chocolate-hazelnut spread

3 large egg whites

½ cup sugar

5 ounces Perugina Baci or other chocolate-hazelnut truffles, finely chopped, plus more for serving

1. Put a medium bowl in the freezer to chill. Line an 8½ x 4½-inch loaf pan with a large sheet of plastic wrap, letting the plastic hang over the sides.

2. Heat ¼ cup of the cream in a small saucepan until warm. Remove from the heat. Add the Nutella and whisk until smooth. Let cool until tepid. Wash and dry the whisk well.

3. In the top part of a double boiler, over barely simmering water, constantly whisk the egg whites and sugar together until the sugar is dissolved and the mixture is opaque and hot but not cooked (the whites will begin to set), 3 to 5 minutes. Remove from the heat. Using an electric mixer on high speed, beat until the whites form very stiff, shiny peaks. Using a rubber spatula, fold about one-quarter of the whites into the Nutella mixture to loosen it.

4. Using the same beaters, whip the remaining ¾ cup cream in the chilled bowl until it forms very stiff peaks. Add the remaining beaten whites and the Nutella mixture to the whipped cream and fold everything together with the spatula. Spread half of the mixture into the loaf pan, smoothing the top, and sprinkle with about two-thirds of the chopped truffles, reserving the remaining truffles as garnish. Spread with the remaining mixture. Cover the top with the overhanging plastic wrap. Freeze until set, at least 4 hours or overnight.

5. To serve, there are two options. For a more formal look, fold back the plastic, invert the pan onto a chilled platter, unmold, and remove the plastic. Slice the semifreddo and transfer each slice to a chilled dessert plate. Or spoon the semifreddo directly from the pan (watch out for the plastic wrap) into chilled ice cream bowls. Sprinkle each serving with the remaining truffles and serve immediately.

✳ ✳ ✳ Love and Baci ✳ ✳ ✳

I didn't grow up eating Snickers bars or Twix. In our house, we ate imported Italian candy. Every Valentine's Day, my father would give us all Perugina Baci candy—chocolate hazelnut "kisses"—to show us how much he loved us. I still love those truffles, and thankfully, you can find them at specialty groceries now, like Trader Joe's.

La Pacchia è Finita!

La pacchia è finita is a famous phrase in Italian that means the fun has ended, the party's over, and it's time to go home. But it's not sad. *Pacchia* is a state of mind where you don't worry, but are happy. It's about the good life. *Che pacchia!* is the same as saying something is easy, like a piece of cake.

And so I'm leaving you with that thought: that you can live the good life no matter where or who you are. We get out of life what we put into it, and I hope you receive as much love and sweetness as you've all given to me.

One final Italian proverb: *A tavola non si invecchia.* It means, "At the table with good friends and family, you do not become old." I'm raising my glass to all of us staying young in our hearts, our minds, and our love—even if we can't keep some other parts from sagging just a little!

Tanti Baci,

Teresa xx

Index

Fabulicious! On The Grill